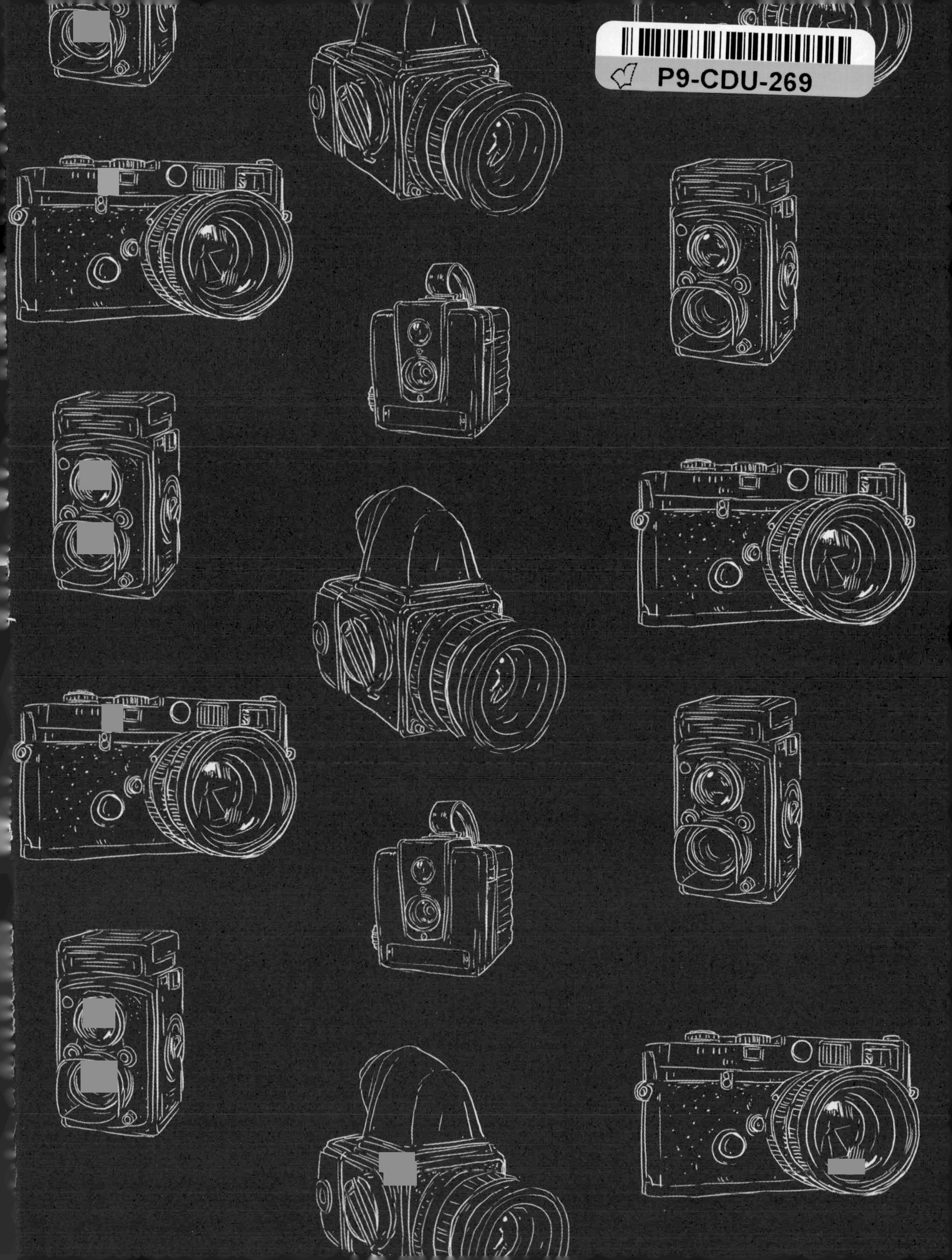

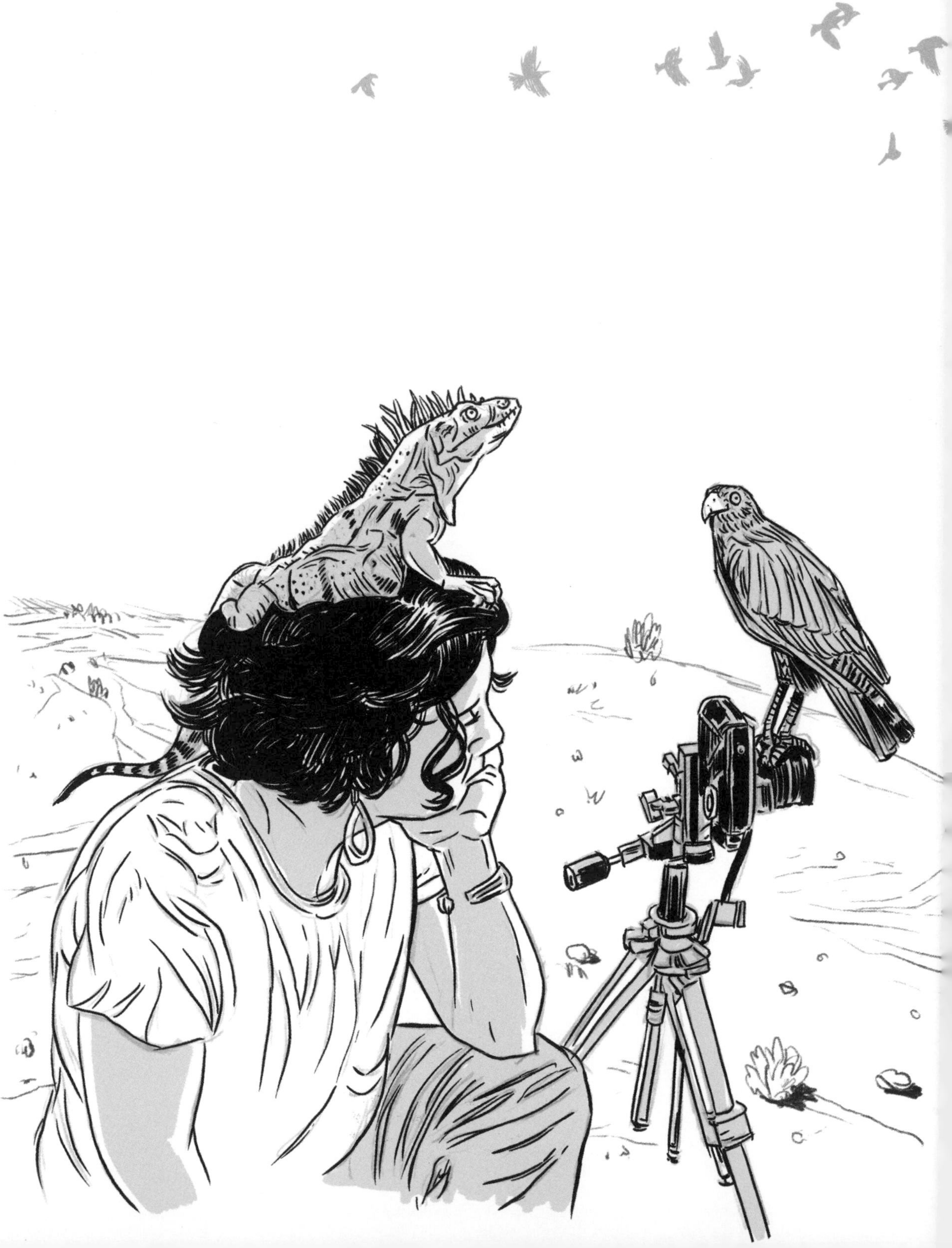

PHOTOGRAPHIC
THE LIFE OF GRACIELA ITURBIDE
ISABEL QUINTERO + ZEKE PEÑA

The J. Paul Getty Museum, Los Angeles

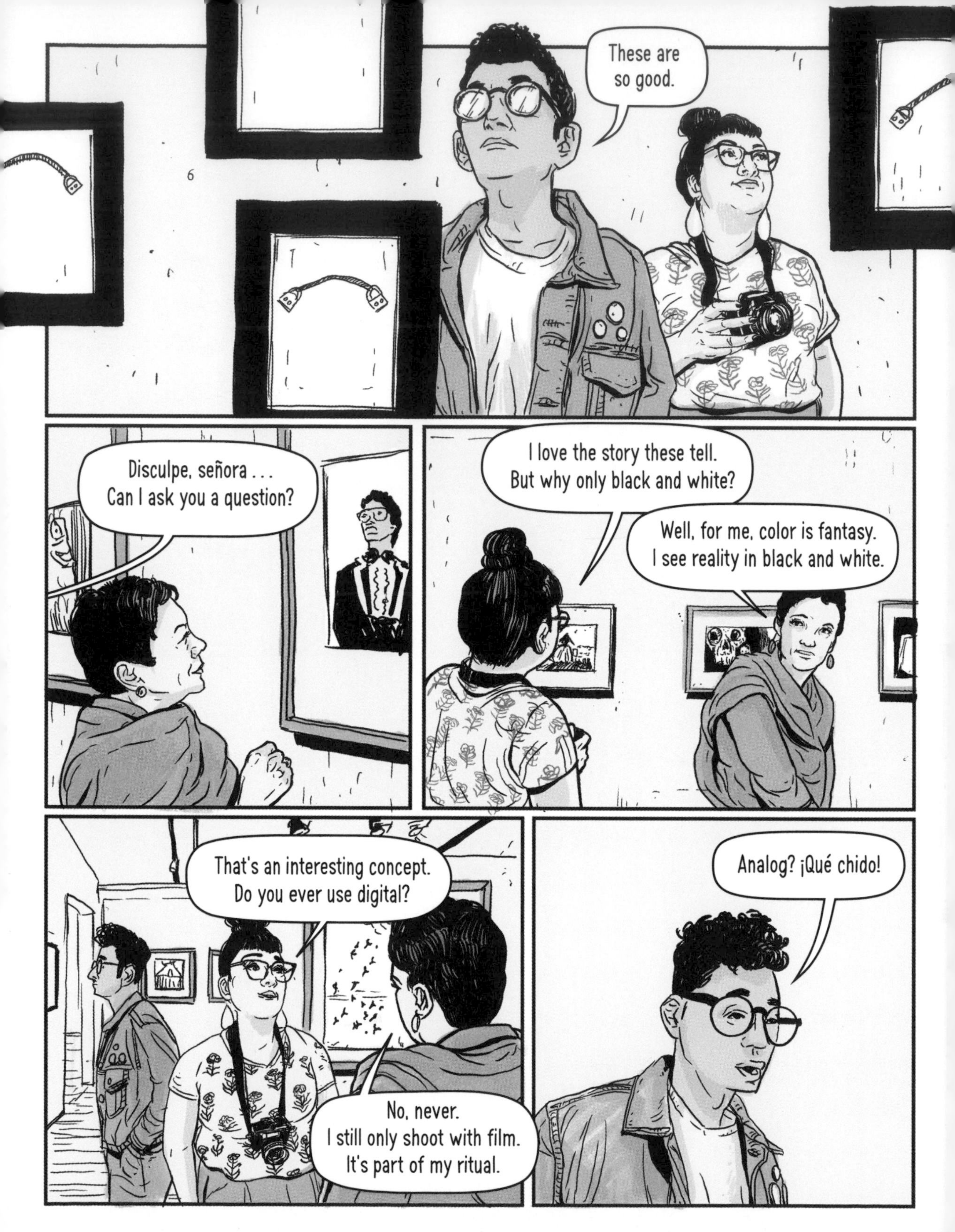
These are so good.
Disculpe, señora . . . Can I ask you a question?
I love the story these tell. But why only black and white?
Well, for me, color is fantasy. I see reality in black and white.
That's an interesting concept. Do you ever use digital?
No, never. I still only shoot with film. It's part of my ritual.
Analog? ¡Qué chido!

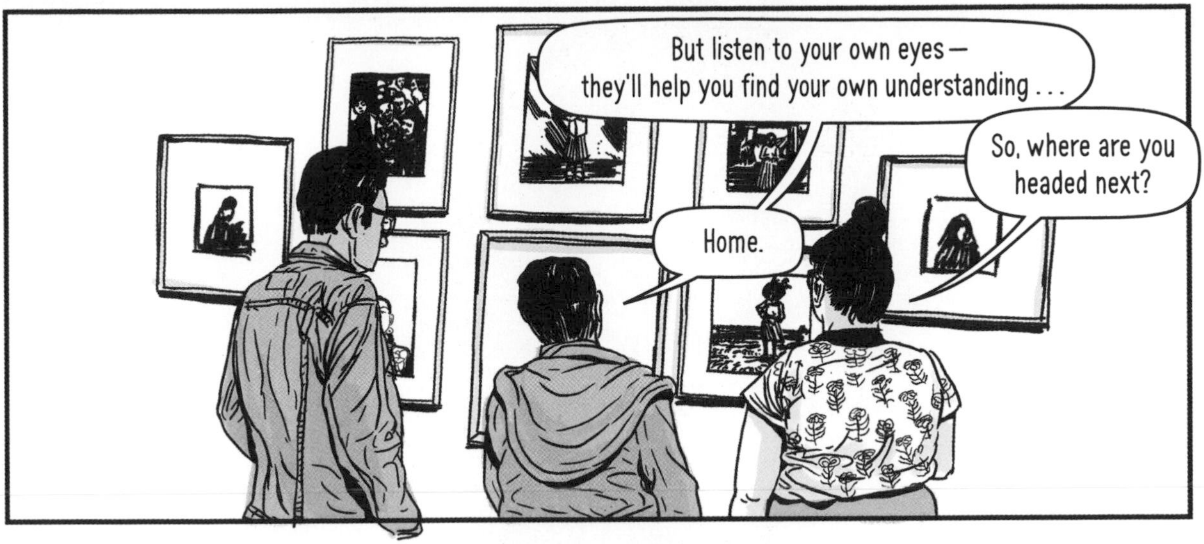
But listen to your own eyes—
they'll help you find your own understanding . . .
Home.
So, where are you headed next?

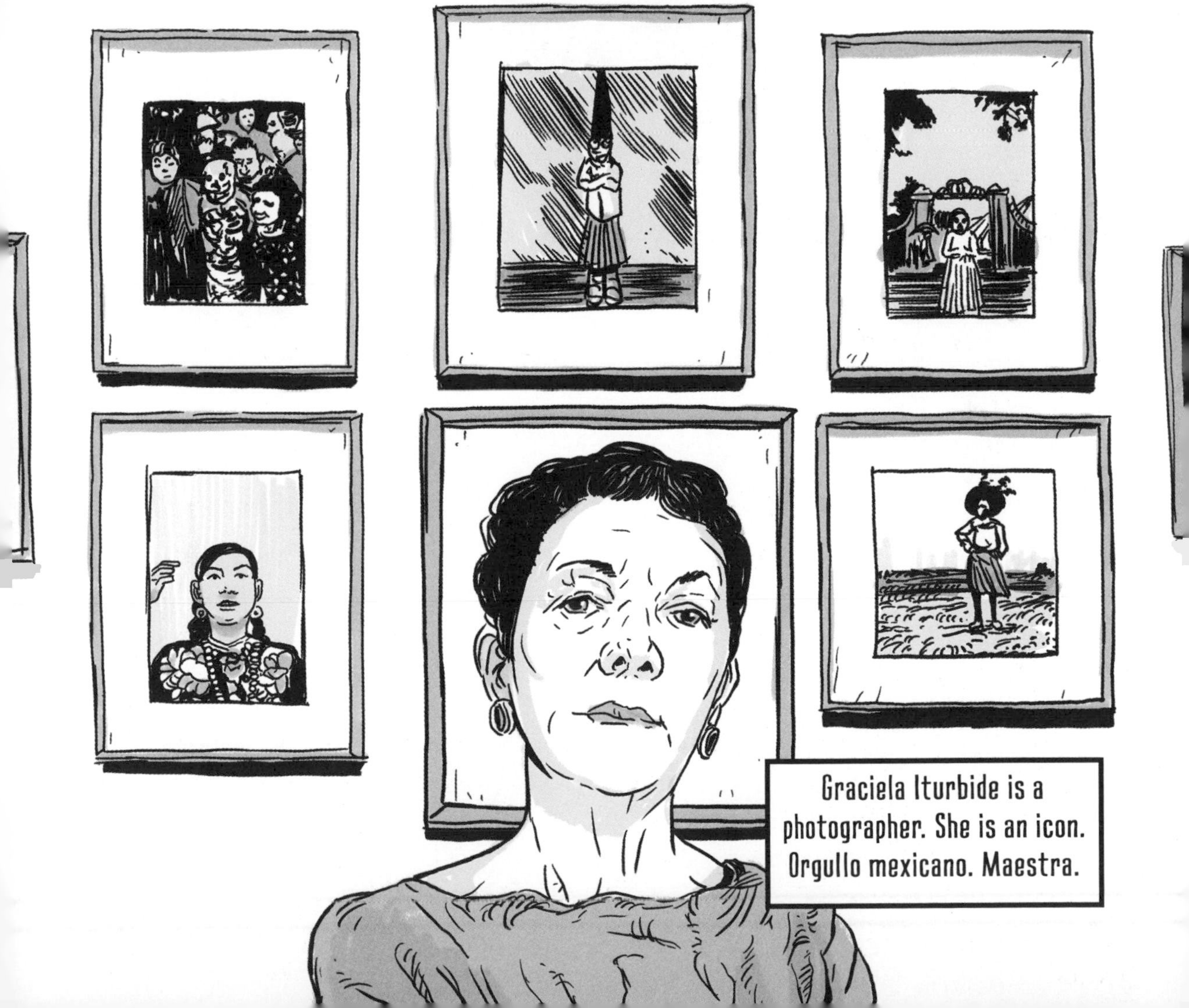
Graciela Iturbide is a photographer. She is an icon. Orgullo mexicano. Maestra.

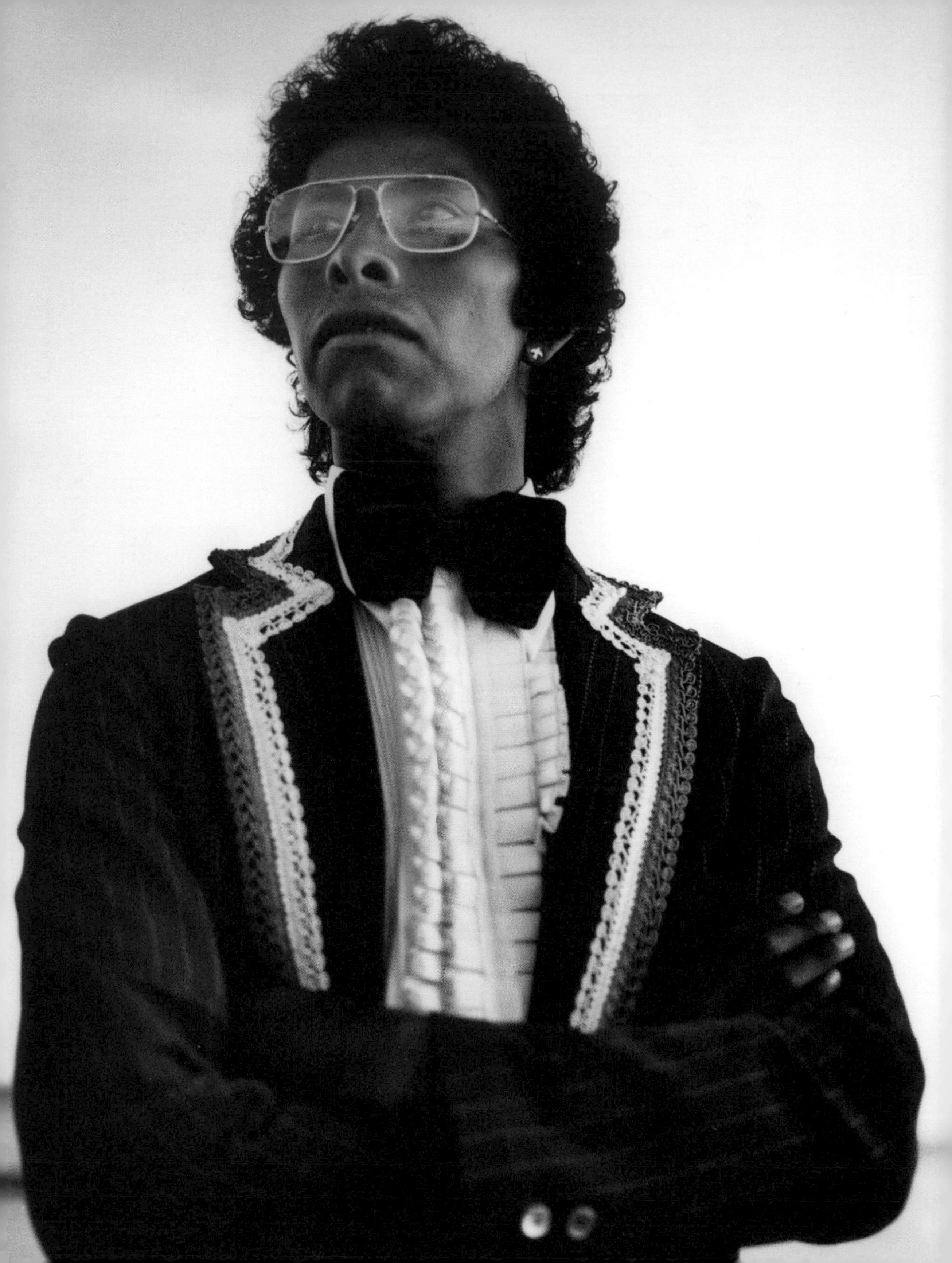

LET'S BEGIN this photographic journey in northern Mexico, where Western culture and commerce transformed the once-nomadic Seris, the indigenous people of the Sonoran Desert. Where Graciela Iturbide was assigned her first major commission by the Instituto Nacional Indigenista. It's as good a place as any.

This story, Reader, is a piecing together of Graciela's life. It is a kaleidoscopic unraveling of almost five decades behind the camera. Of countless awards and exhibitions. In these pages, all the events are in order and none are in order. Is that not as it should be? It is in black and white because color is fantasy. Graciela captures reality in black and white. In the following pages, Reader, when you are admiring her beautiful and compelling and sometimes disturbing work, do not think words like magical or surreal—her images are as real as they get. Here is her story.

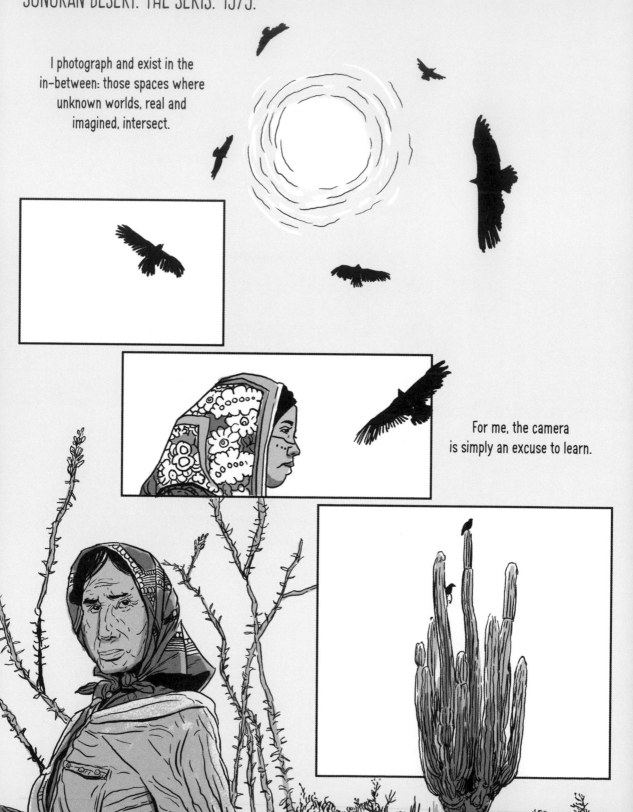

SONORAN DESERT. THE SERIS. 1979.

I photograph and exist in the in-between: those spaces where unknown worlds, real and imagined, intersect.

For me, the camera is simply an excuse to learn.

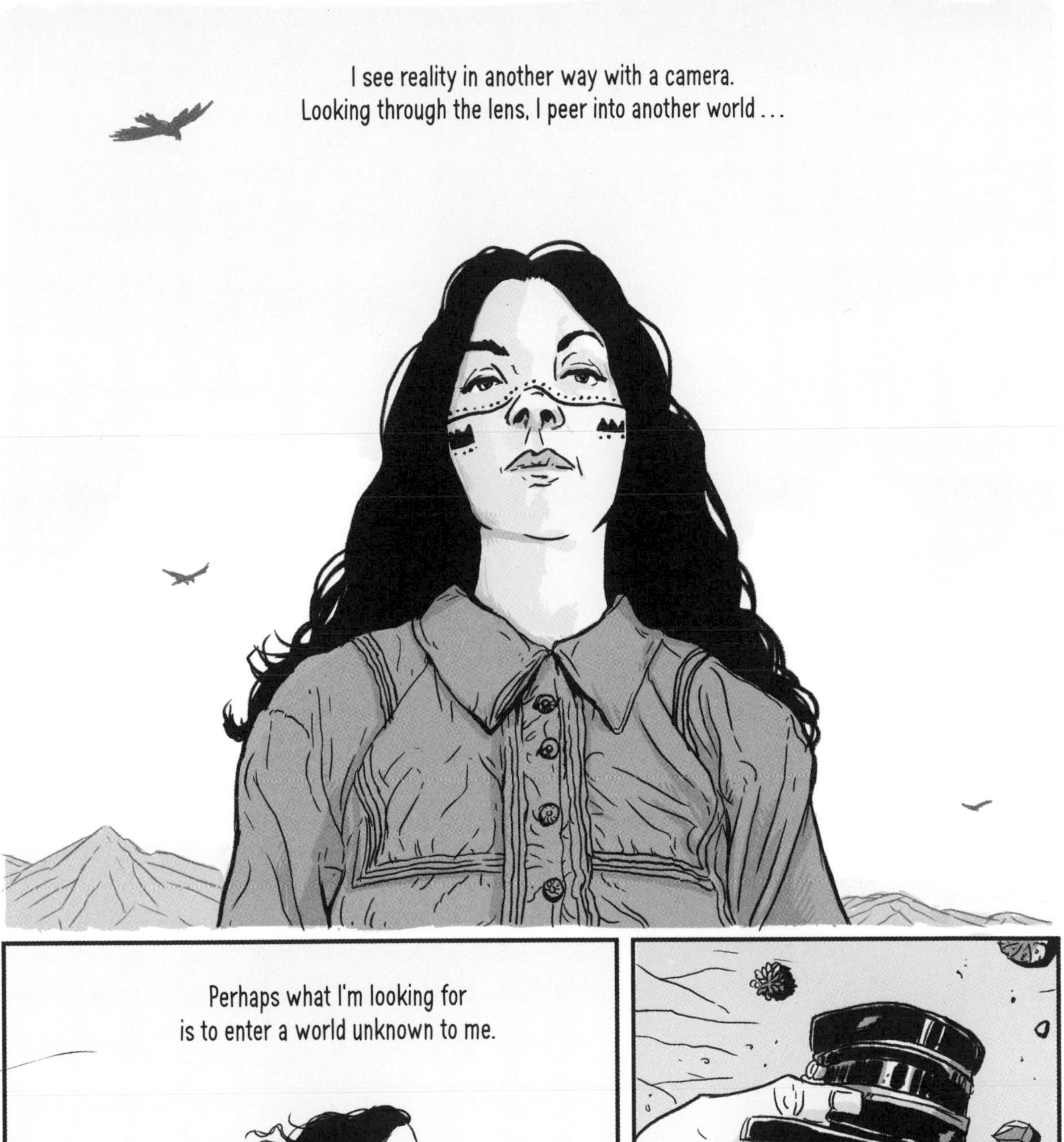
I see reality in another way with a camera.
Looking through the lens, I peer into another world . . .

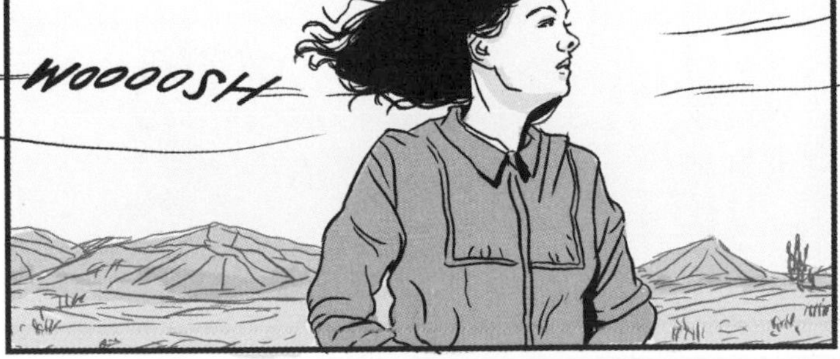
Perhaps what I'm looking for
is to enter a world unknown to me.
WOOOOSH

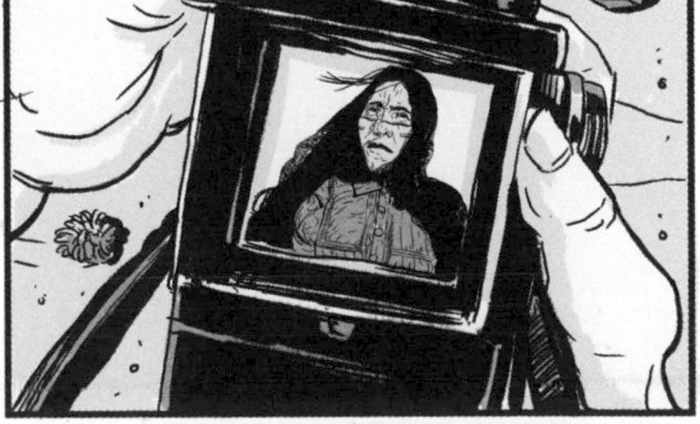

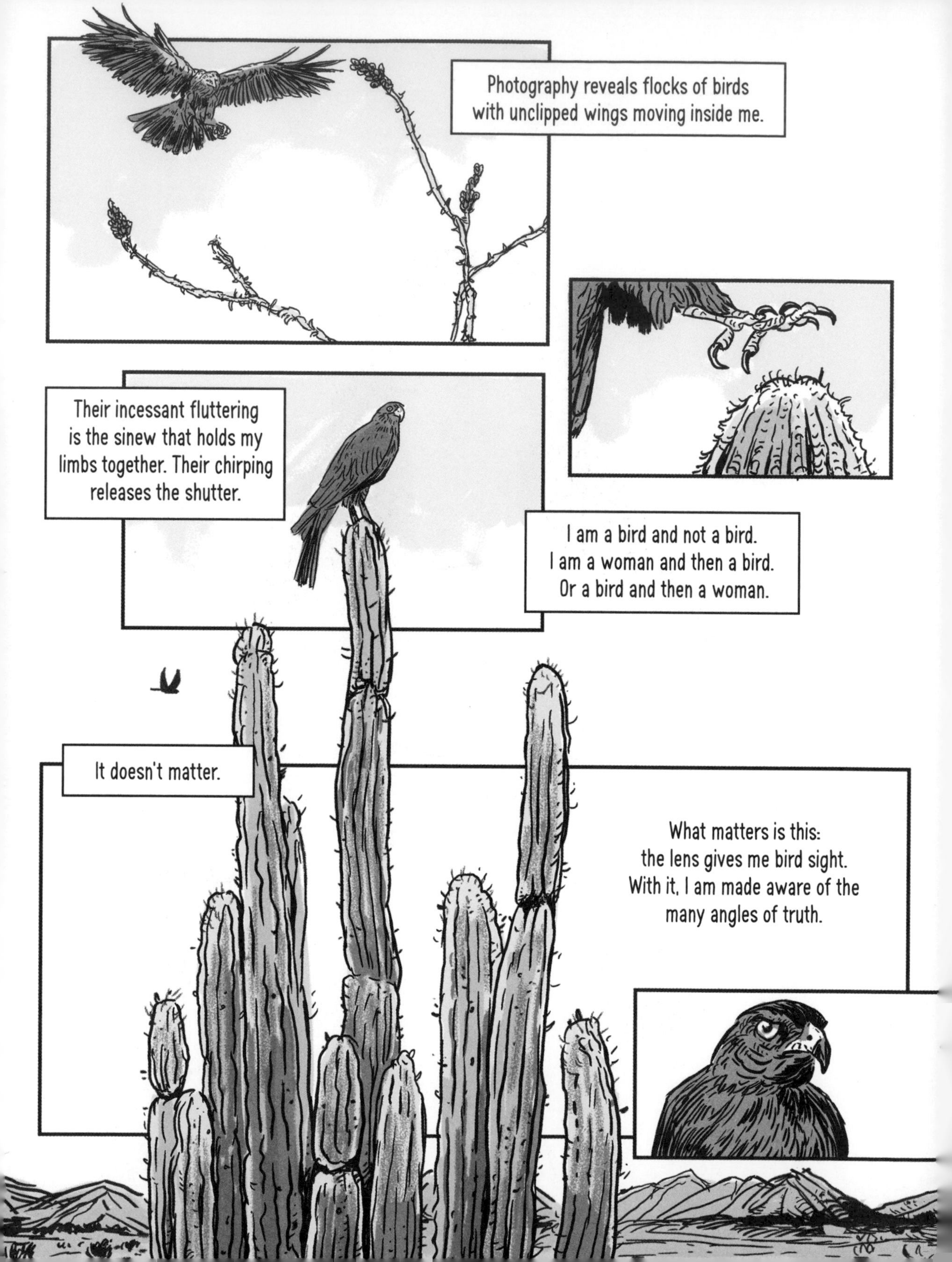

Photography reveals flocks of birds with unclipped wings moving inside me.
Their incessant fluttering is the sinew that holds my limbs together. Their chirping releases the shutter.
I am a bird and not a bird. I am a woman and then a bird. Or a bird and then a woman.
It doesn't matter.
What matters is this: the lens gives me bird sight. With it, I am made aware of the many angles of truth.

A life, a rock, a country exists in the reality that I imagine.
Isn't that a powerful thing? Creating truth? The still image is suspended reality.

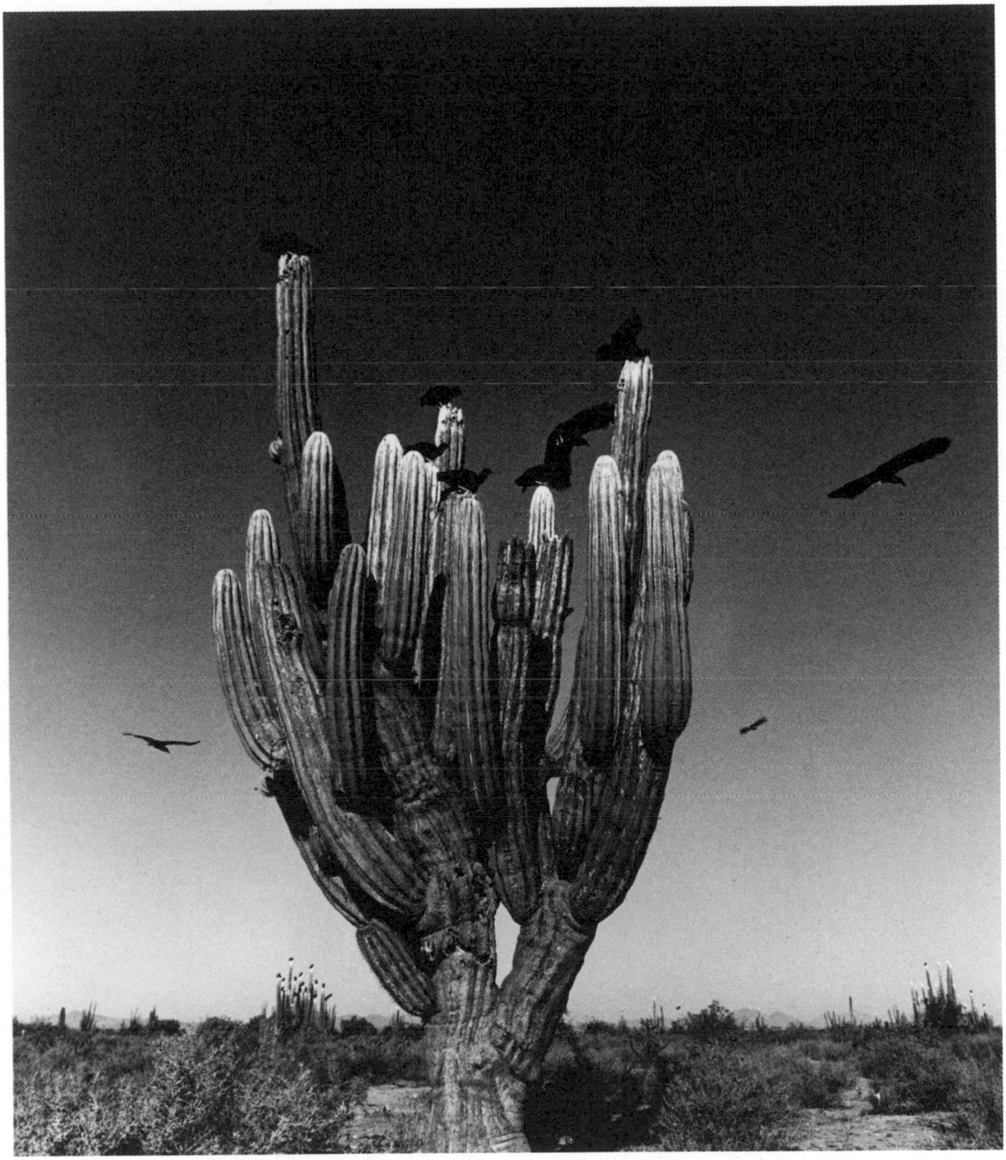

This is how I've learned to use my bird sight.
But it hasn't always been like this.

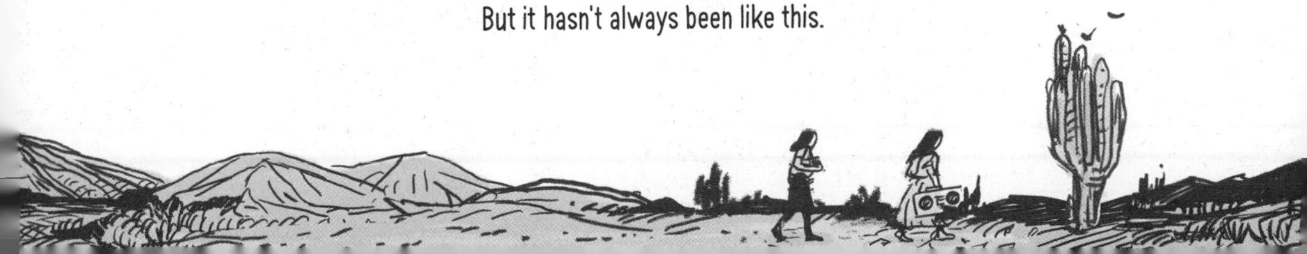

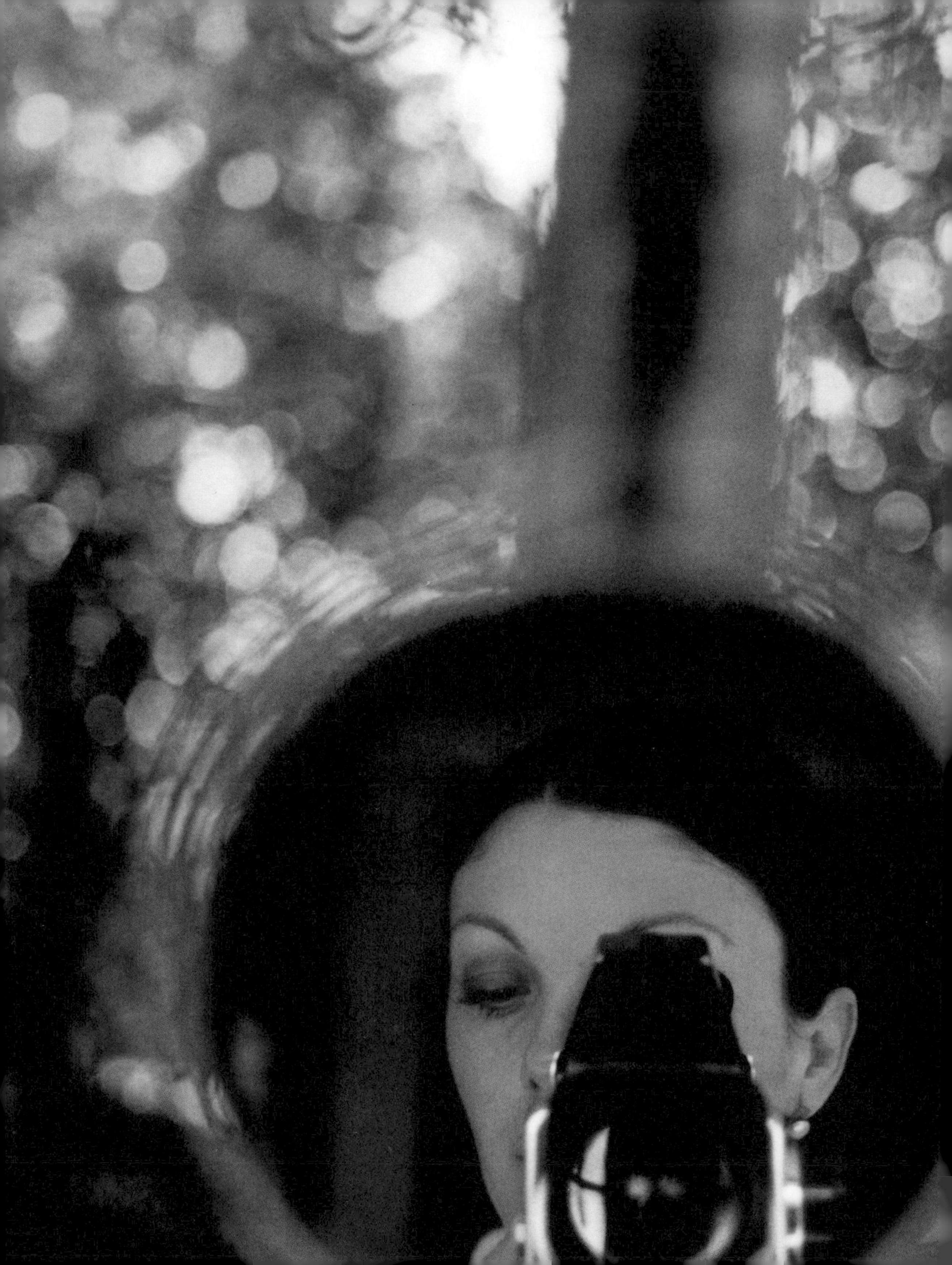

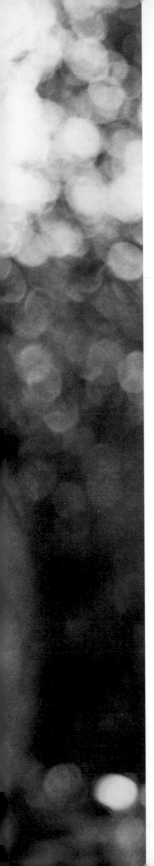

LET'S GO BACK to the very beginning, when Graciela
was a little girl. Before the awards and the exhibitions.
Before she met the famous photographer Manuel
Álvarez Bravo, before she met the painter Francisco
Toledo, and way before she went into the Sonoran
Desert to photograph the Seris. In this land of Before,
Graciela had no great adventures; nothing was unknown.
The eldest daughter of a well-to-do family, she lived in a
world where expectations were set and not questioned.
Where you were told, "Believe in God, marry, have
children, keep a home," and you obeyed. That is what
Graciela did, marrying and having three children in her
early twenties.

But like all birds who are put in cages, even ornate ones,
she was restless.

Paving your own path comes with sacrifice, Reader. Do
you know how painful sacrifice can be? Graciela gave up
a life of comfort and convention—choosing instead the
path of the artist and risking everything.

Not all women artists have enjoyed the freedom that
she has. Graciela knows she has been lucky, and she
doesn't take her opportunities for granted.

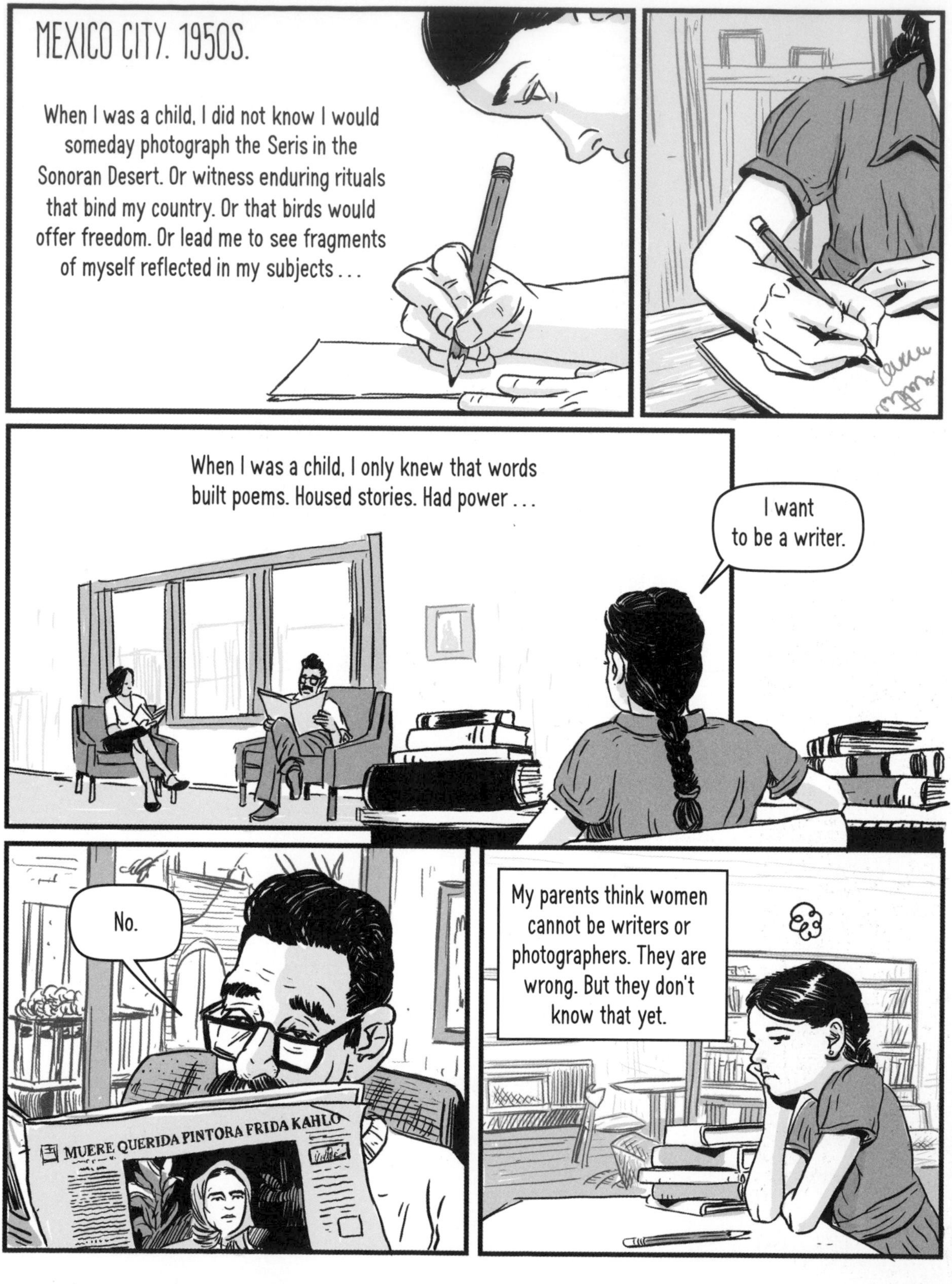
MEXICO CITY. 1950S.
When I was a child, I did not know I would someday photograph the Seris in the Sonoran Desert. Or witness enduring rituals that bind my country. Or that birds would offer freedom. Or lead me to see fragments of myself reflected in my subjects . . .
When I was a child, I only knew that words built poems. Housed stories. Had power . . .
I want to be a writer.
No.
MUERE QUERIDA PINTORA FRIDA KAHLO
My parents think women cannot be writers or photographers. They are wrong. But they don't know that yet.

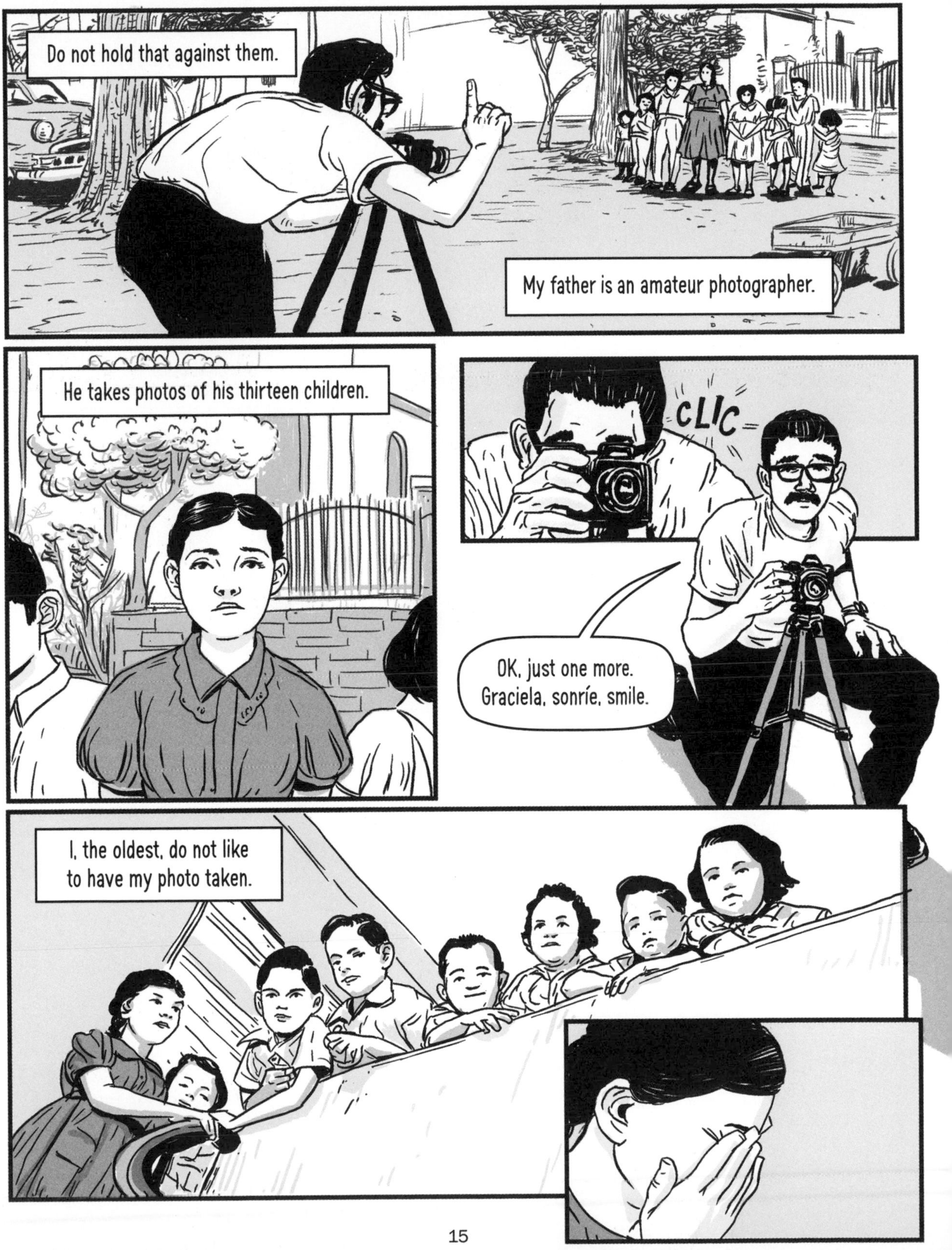

Do not hold that against them.
My father is an amateur photographer.
He takes photos of his thirteen children.
CLIC
OK, just one more.
Graciela, sonríe, smile.
I, the oldest, do not like
to have my photo taken.

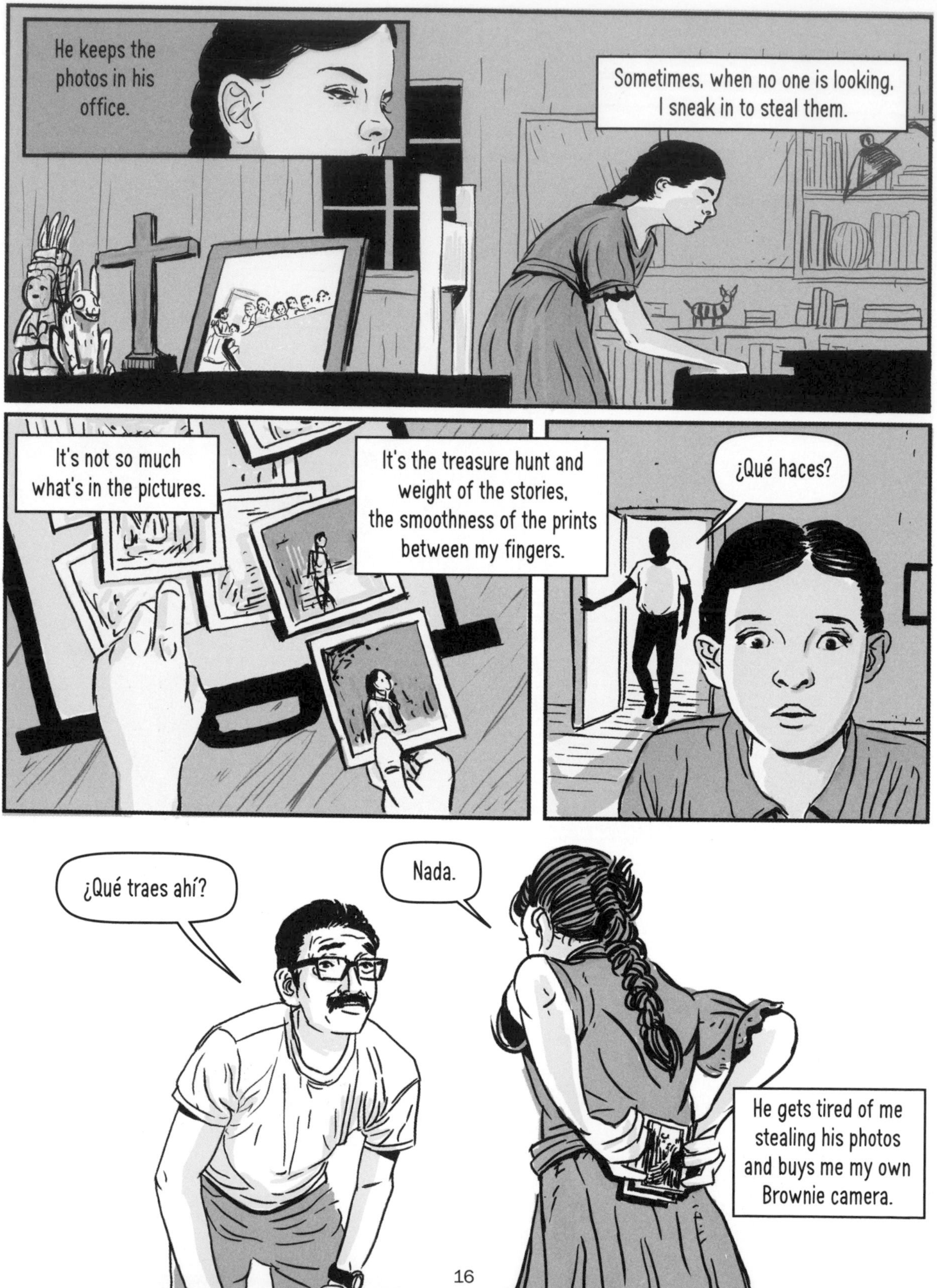
He keeps the photos in his office.
Sometimes, when no one is looking, I sneak in to steal them.
It's not so much what's in the pictures.
It's the treasure hunt and weight of the stories, the smoothness of the prints between my fingers.
¿Qué haces?
¿Qué traes ahí?
Nada.
He gets tired of me stealing his photos and buys me my own Brownie camera.

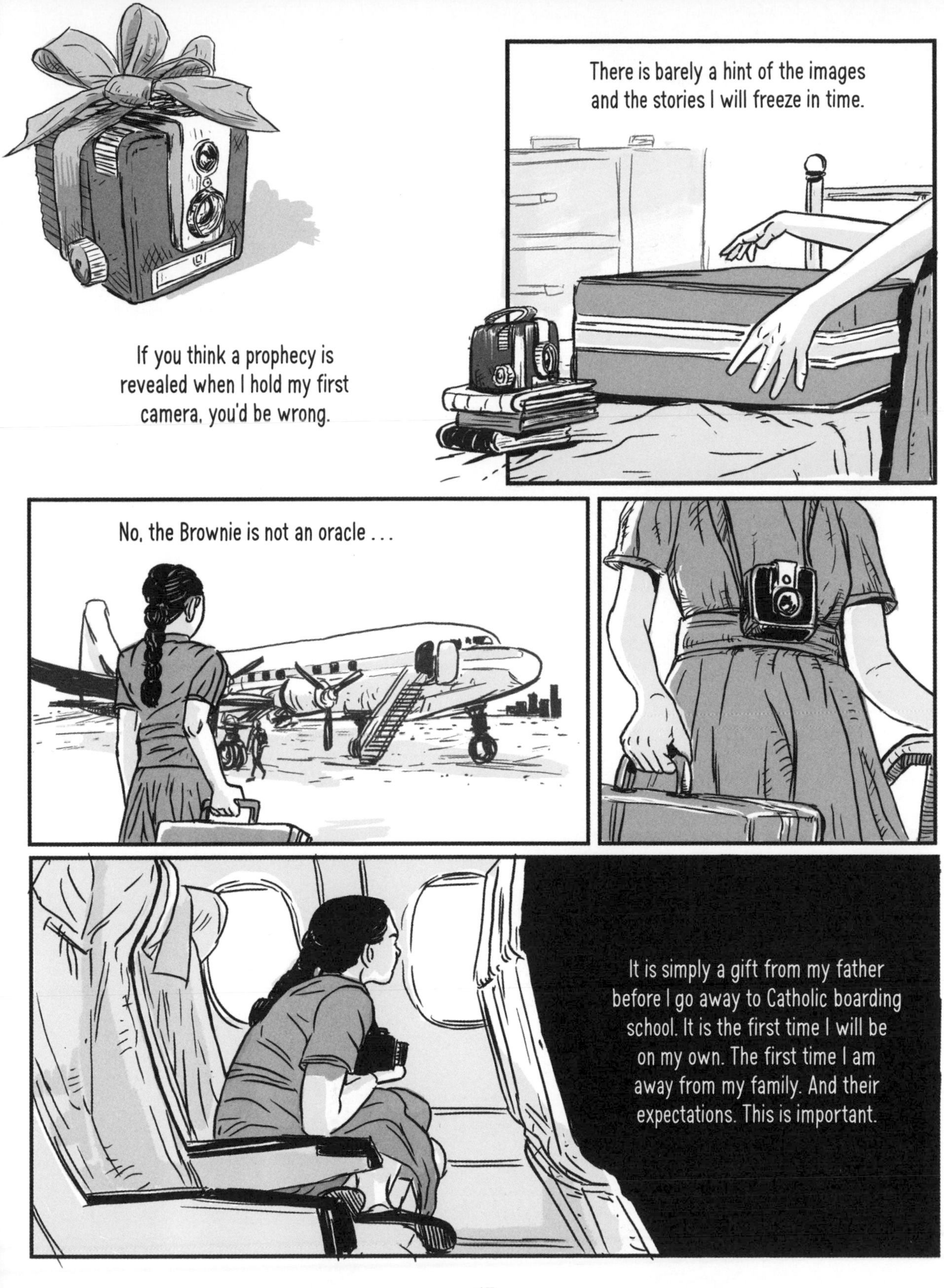
If you think a prophecy is revealed when I hold my first camera, you'd be wrong.
There is barely a hint of the images and the stories I will freeze in time.
No, the Brownie is not an oracle . . .
It is simply a gift from my father before I go away to Catholic boarding school. It is the first time I will be on my own. The first time I am away from my family. And their expectations. This is important.

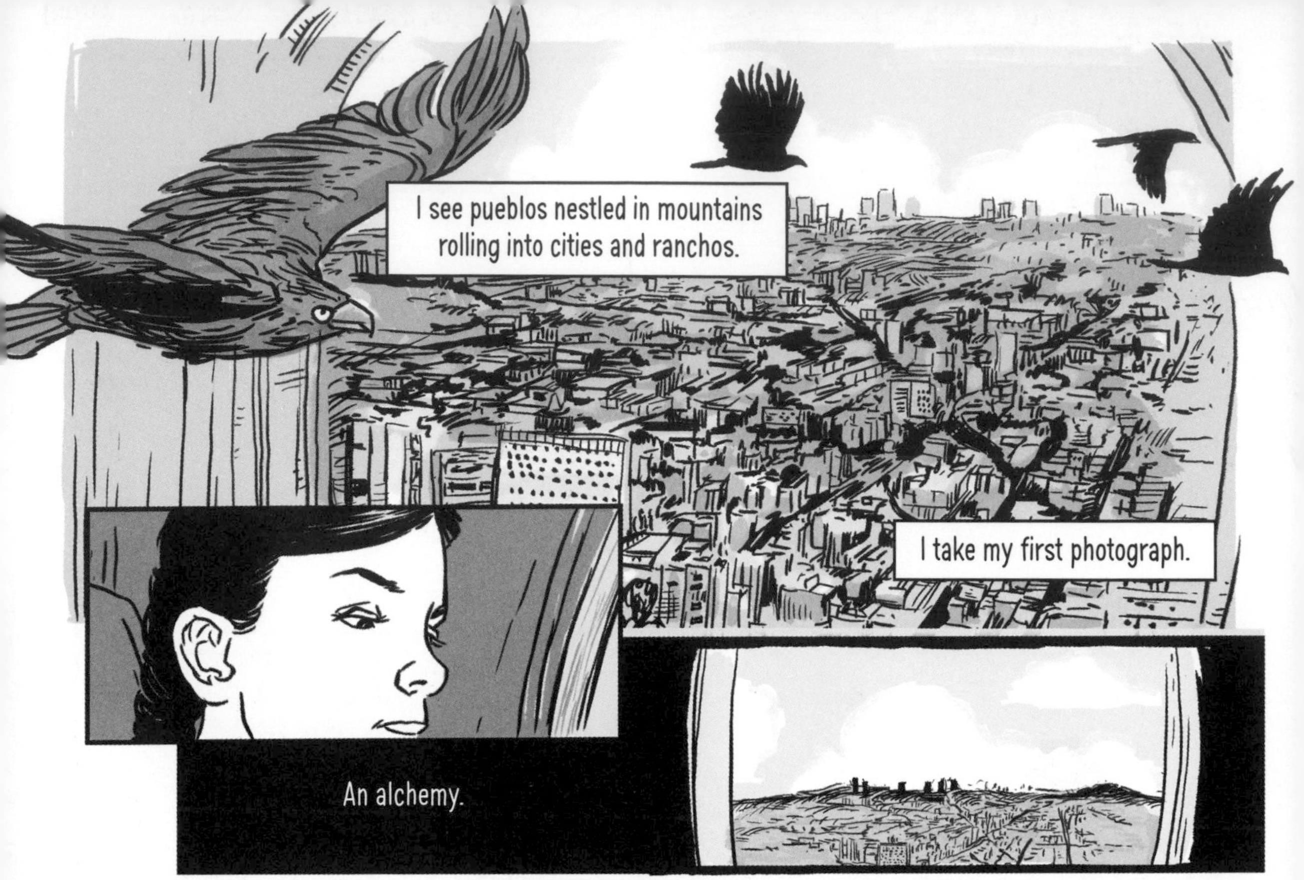
I see pueblos nestled in mountains rolling into cities and ranchos.
I take my first photograph.
An alchemy.

I become bird in the heavens
and am filled with birds.
The camera awakens wings.
The wings give me new eyes.

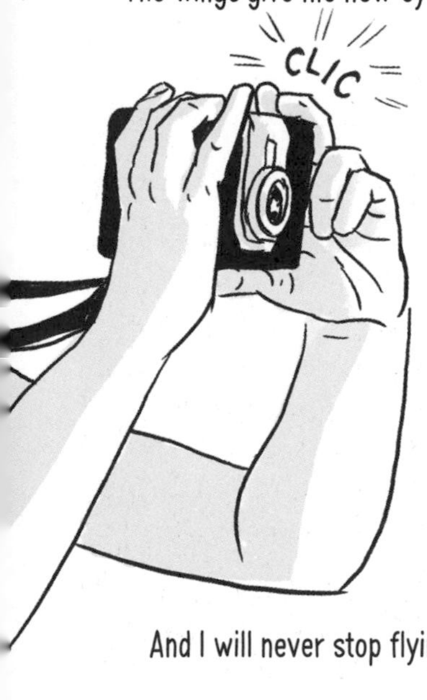
CLIC

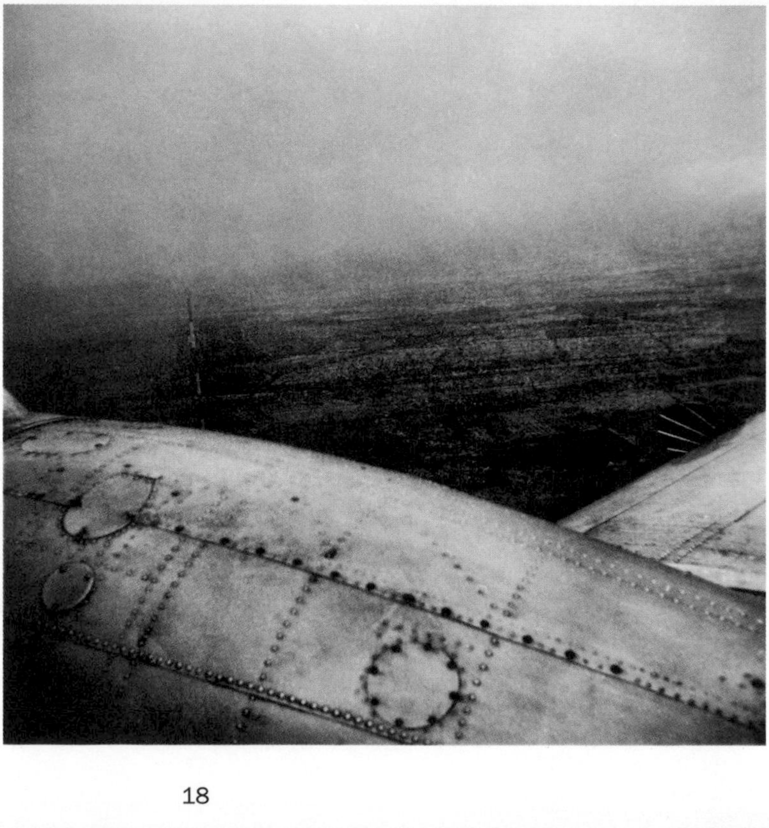

And I will never stop flying.

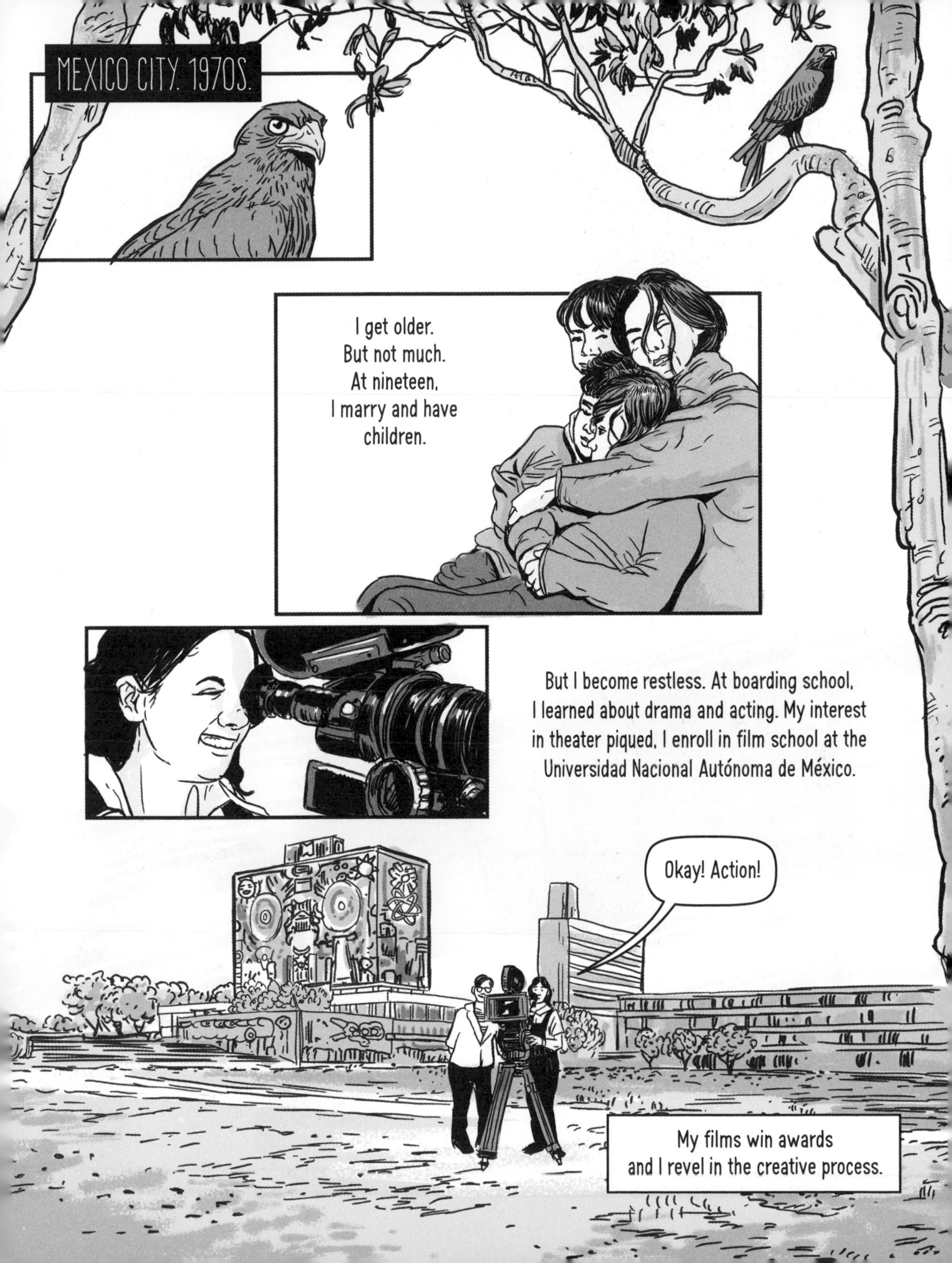
MEXICO CITY. 1970S.
I get older. But not much. At nineteen, I marry and have children.
But I become restless. At boarding school, I learned about drama and acting. My interest in theater piqued, I enroll in film school at the Universidad Nacional Autónoma de México.
Okay! Action!
My films win awards and I revel in the creative process.

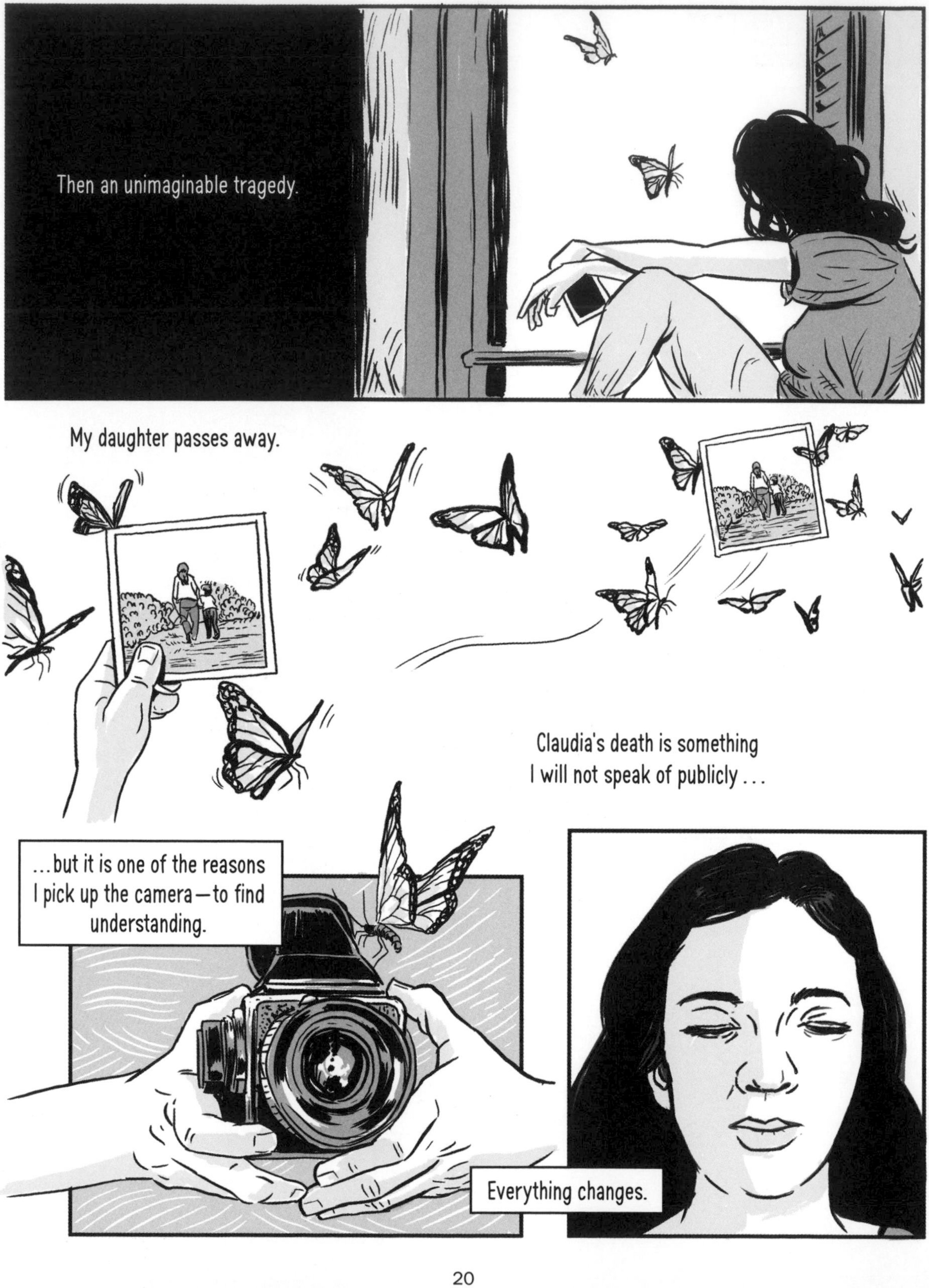
Then an unimaginable tragedy.
My daughter passes away.
Claudia's death is something I will not speak of publicly . . .
. . . but it is one of the reasons I pick up the camera—to find understanding.
Everything changes.

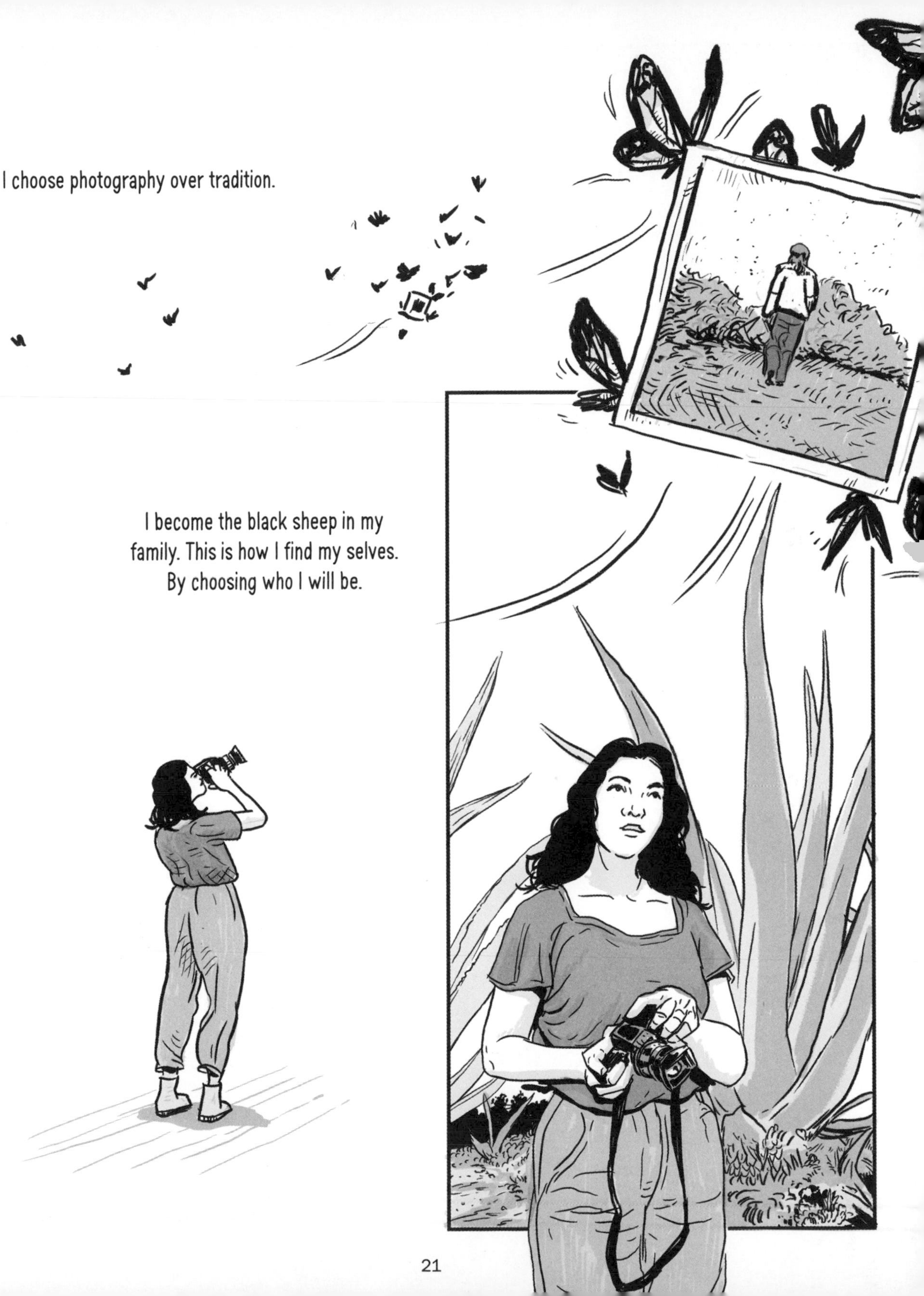
I choose photography over tradition.
I become the black sheep in my family. This is how I find my selves. By choosing who I will be.

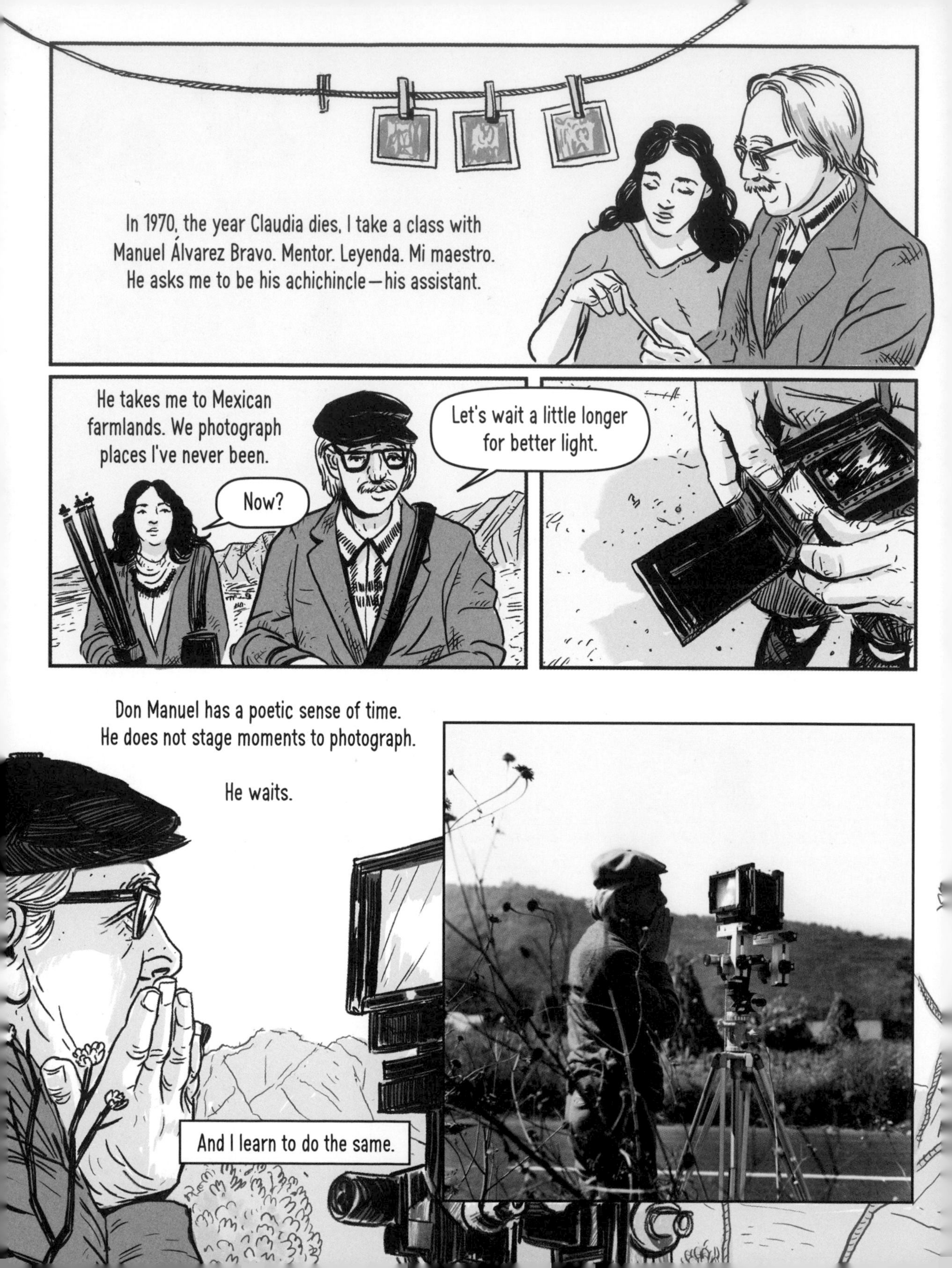
In 1970, the year Claudia dies, I take a class with Manuel Álvarez Bravo. Mentor. Leyenda. Mi maestro. He asks me to be his achichincle—his assistant.
He takes me to Mexican farmlands. We photograph places I've never been.
Now?
Let's wait a little longer for better light.
Don Manuel has a poetic sense of time. He does not stage moments to photograph.
He waits.
And I learn to do the same.

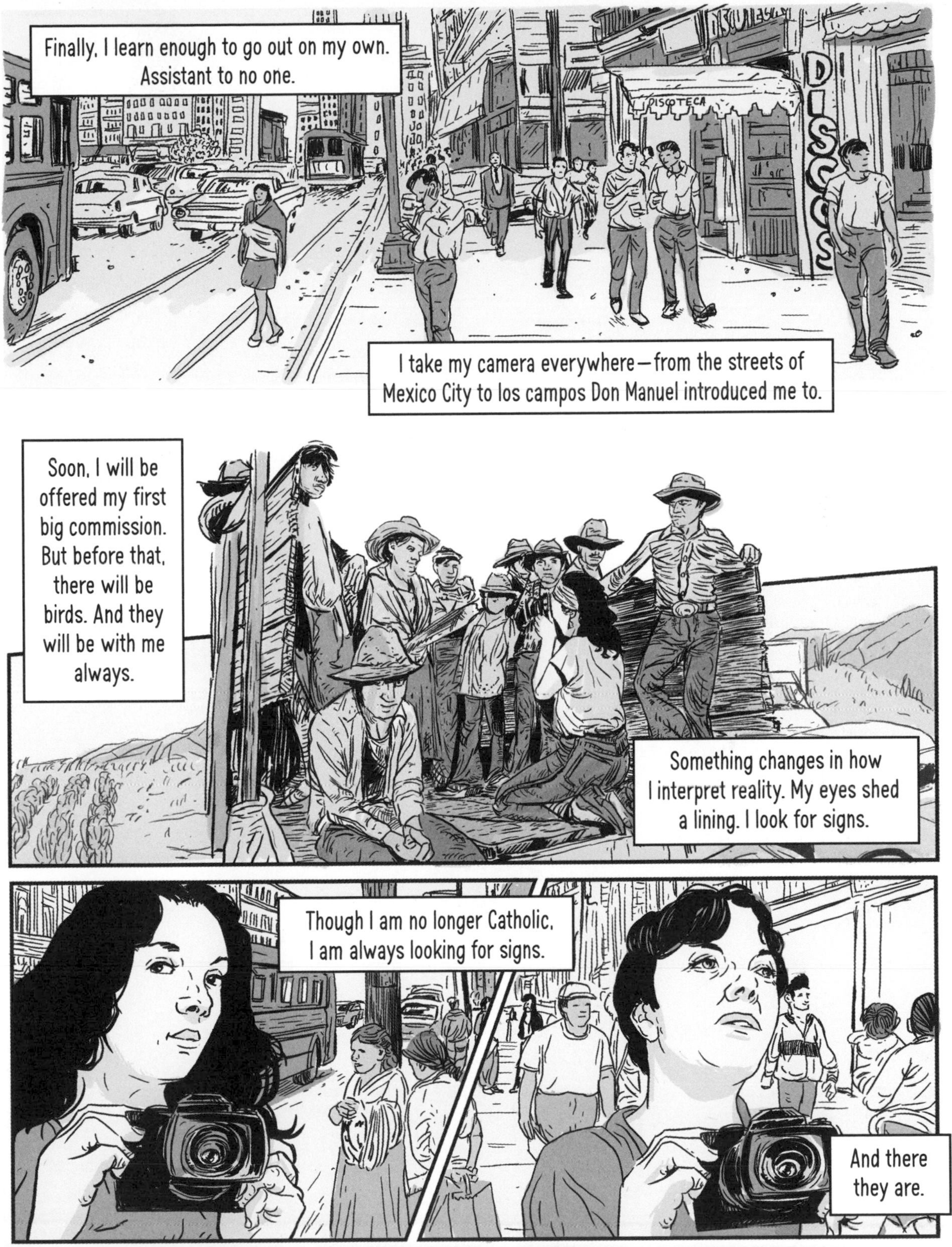
Finally, I learn enough to go out on my own. Assistant to no one.
DISCOTECA
DISCOS
I take my camera everywhere—from the streets of Mexico City to los campos Don Manuel introduced me to.
Soon, I will be offered my first big commission. But before that, there will be birds. And they will be with me always.
Something changes in how I interpret reality. My eyes shed a lining. I look for signs.
Though I am no longer Catholic, I am always looking for signs.
And there they are.

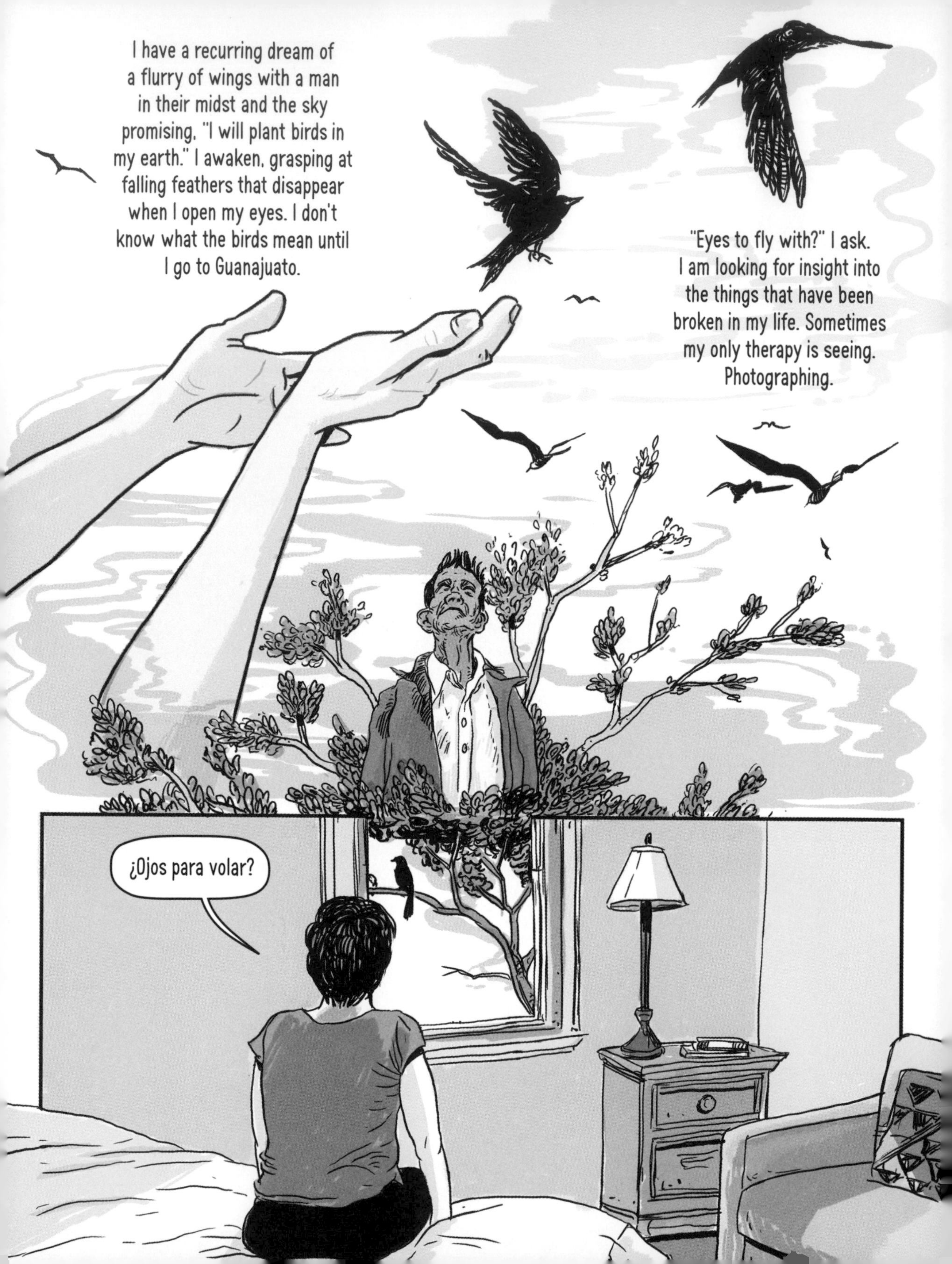
I have a recurring dream of a flurry of wings with a man in their midst and the sky promising, "I will plant birds in my earth." I awaken, grasping at falling feathers that disappear when I open my eyes. I don't know what the birds mean until I go to Guanajuato.
"Eyes to fly with?" I ask. I am looking for insight into the things that have been broken in my life. Sometimes my only therapy is seeing. Photographing.
¿Ojos para volar?

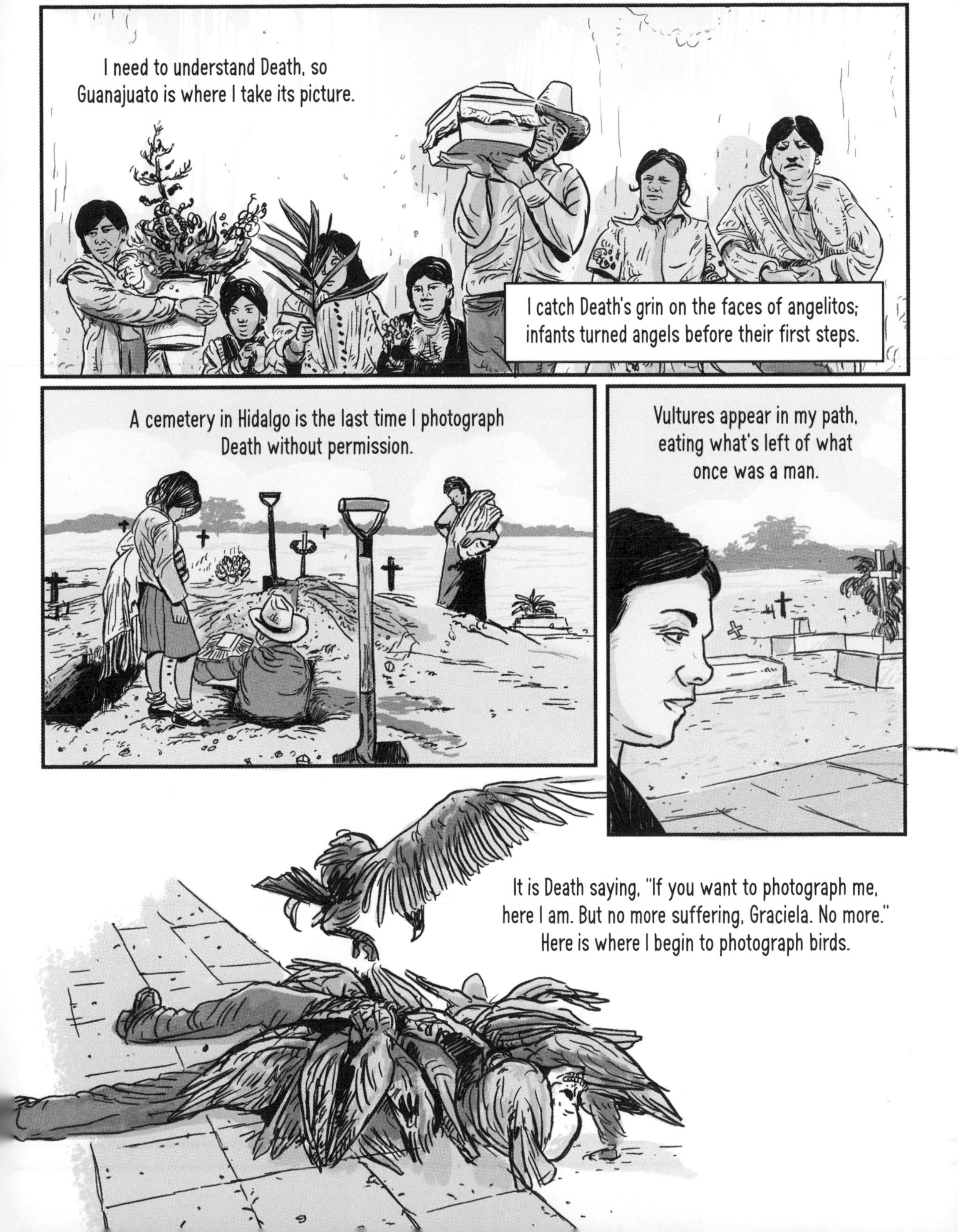
I need to understand Death, so Guanajuato is where I take its picture.
I catch Death's grin on the faces of angelitos; infants turned angels before their first steps.
A cemetery in Hidalgo is the last time I photograph Death without permission.
Vultures appear in my path, eating what's left of what once was a man.
It is Death saying, "If you want to photograph me, here I am. But no more suffering, Graciela. No more."
Here is where I begin to photograph birds.

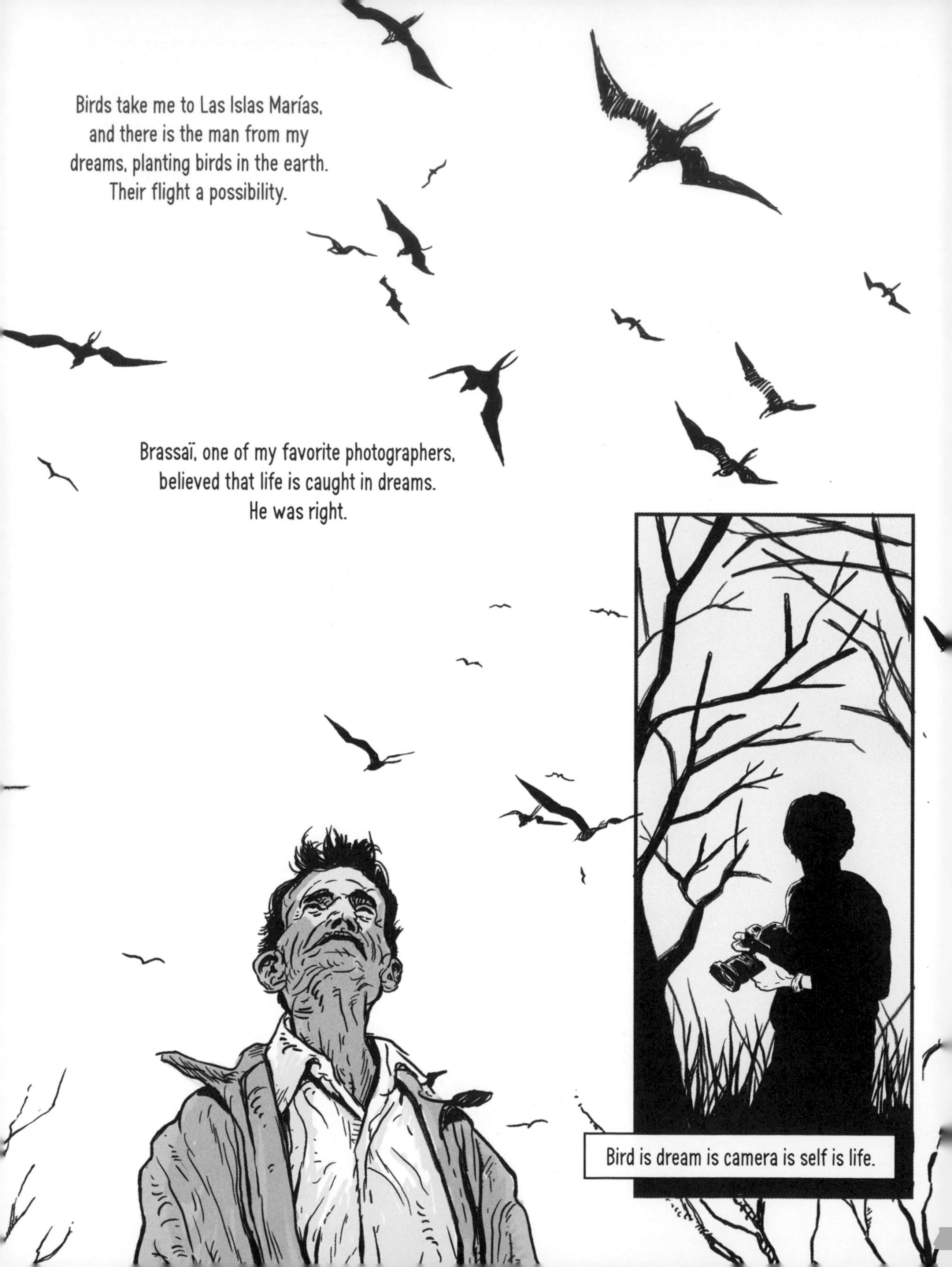
Birds take me to Las Islas Marías, and there is the man from my dreams, planting birds in the earth. Their flight a possibility.
Brassaï, one of my favorite photographers, believed that life is caught in dreams. He was right.
Bird is dream is camera is self is life.

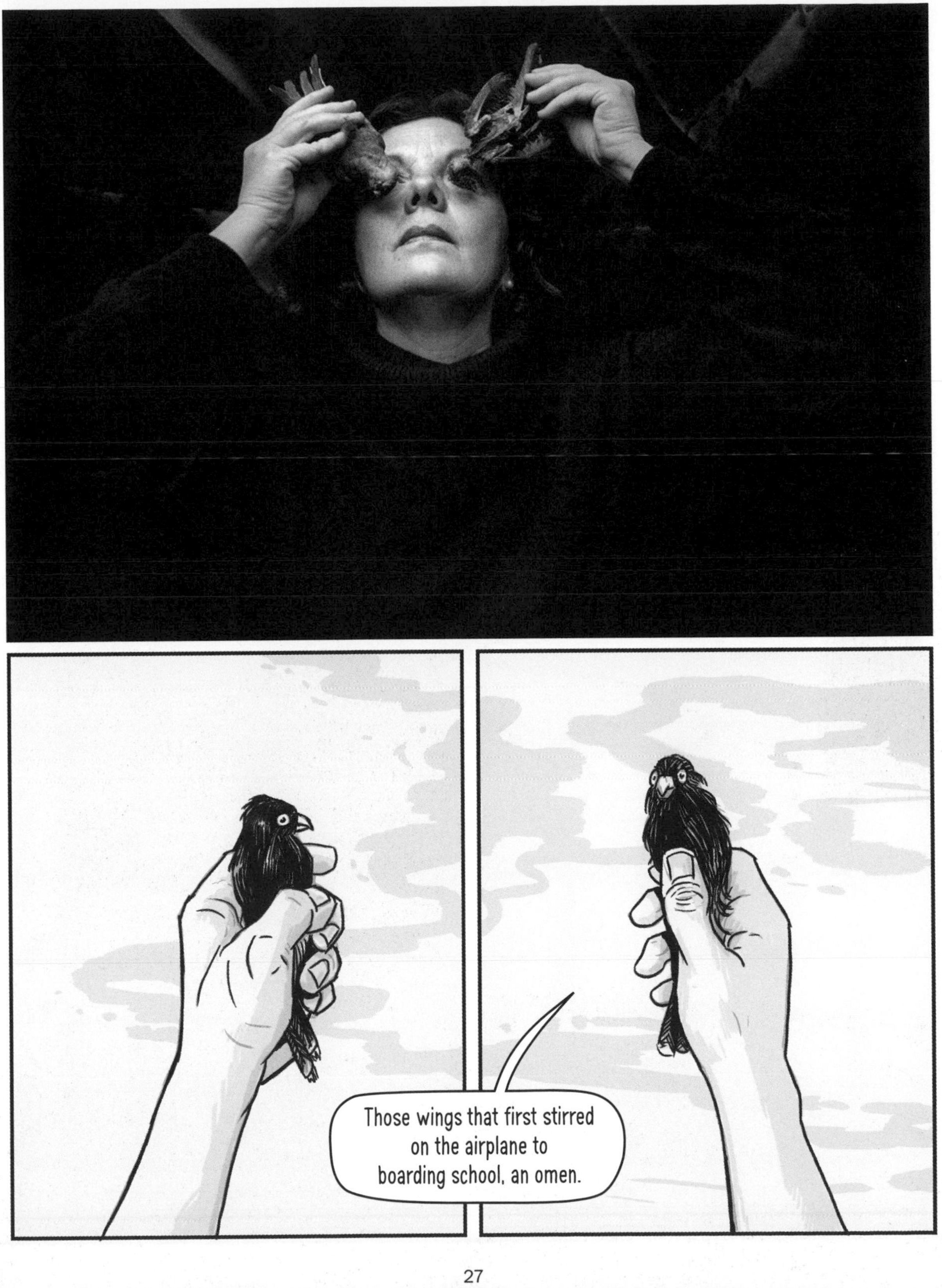
Those wings that first stirred on the airplane to boarding school, an omen.

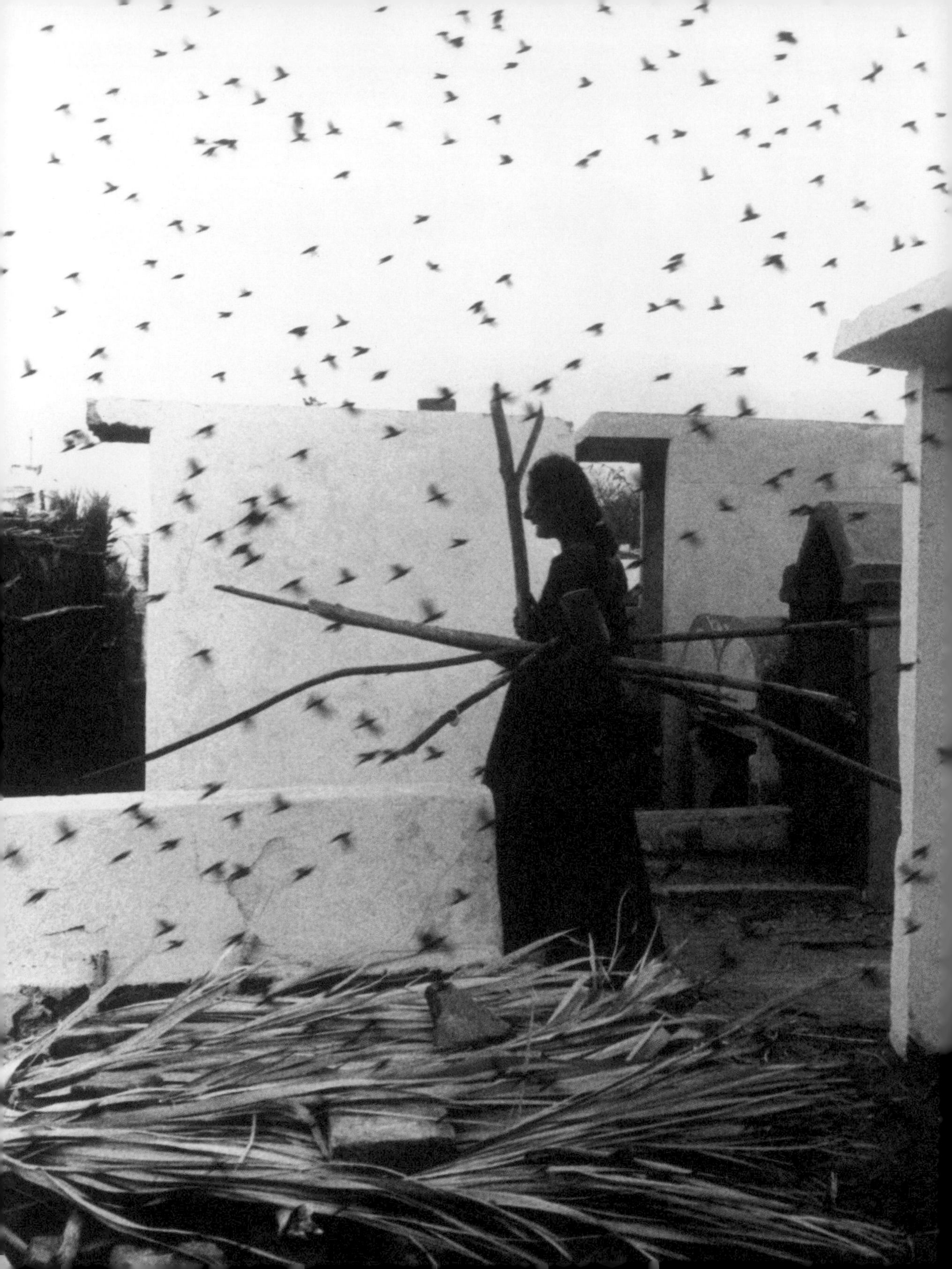

SOME BIRDS are not so lucky. Sometimes Graciela's photographs remind us of lovebirds with clipped wings that continue to sing, their unflinching melancholy a radiant proclamation, a reminder that they were meant to fly.

Graciela's bird sight is compelled by the Mexicans and Mexican Americans living—surviving—in nepantla. The in-between. Ni de aquí, but always searching for a romanticized allá. Members of the White Fence Gang in East Los Angeles dreaming of an America where their mexicanidad is not a reason for marginalization, of a Mexico with no poverty and discrimination. Cholos in Tijuana yearning for an imaginary country, one that accepts everyone, somewhere they can find themselves. And deep in the throbbing heart of Mexico, from Chalma to La Mixteca, Graciela captures la gente enacting rituals pre-Hispanic, Catholic, and in between. Where ritual is survival. How else can culture be held onto?

We, Reader, are unapologetically thrust into that world.

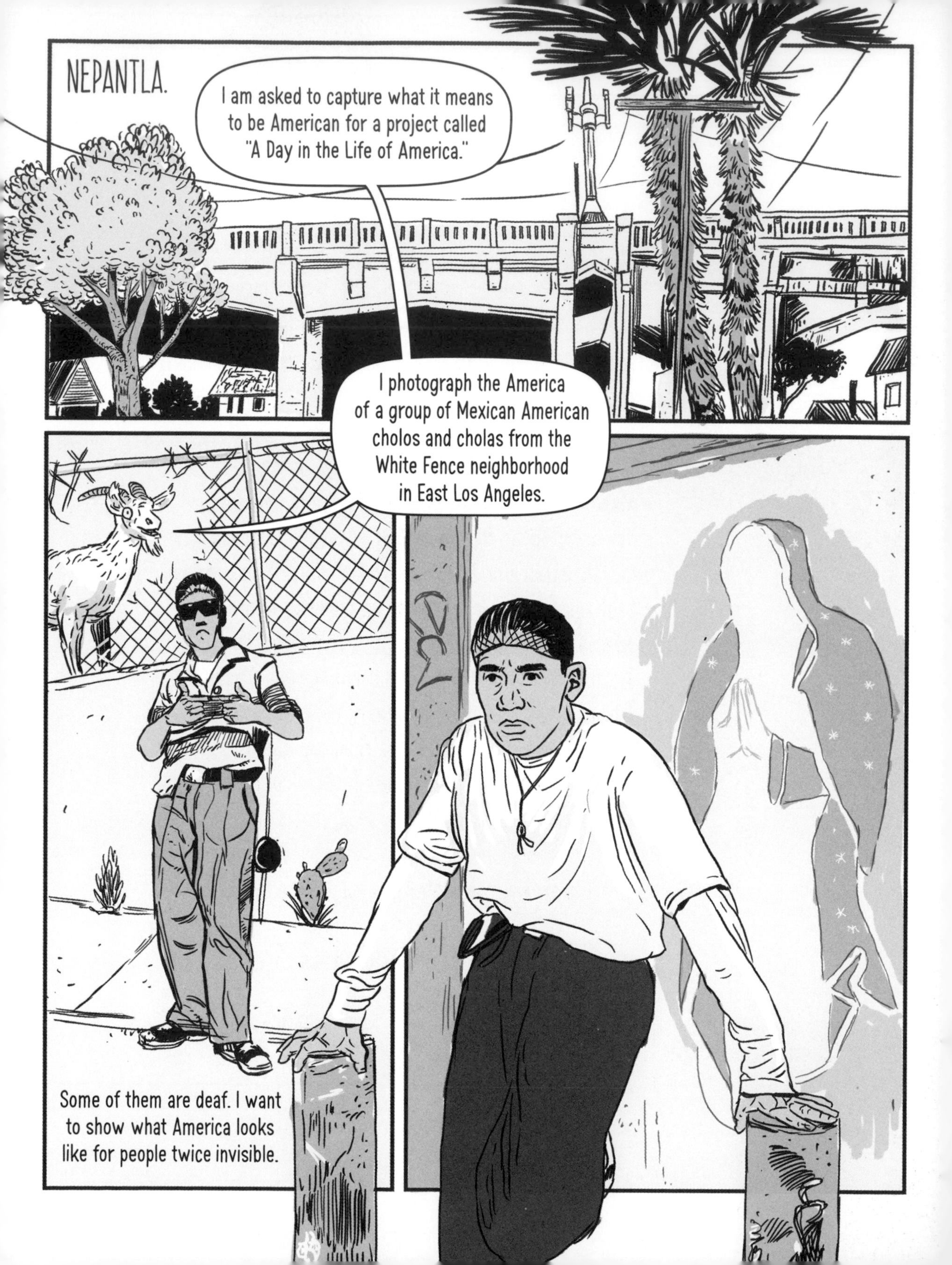
NEPANTLA.
I am asked to capture what it means to be American for a project called "A Day in the Life of America."
I photograph the America of a group of Mexican American cholos and cholas from the White Fence neighborhood in East Los Angeles.
Some of them are deaf. I want to show what America looks like for people twice invisible.

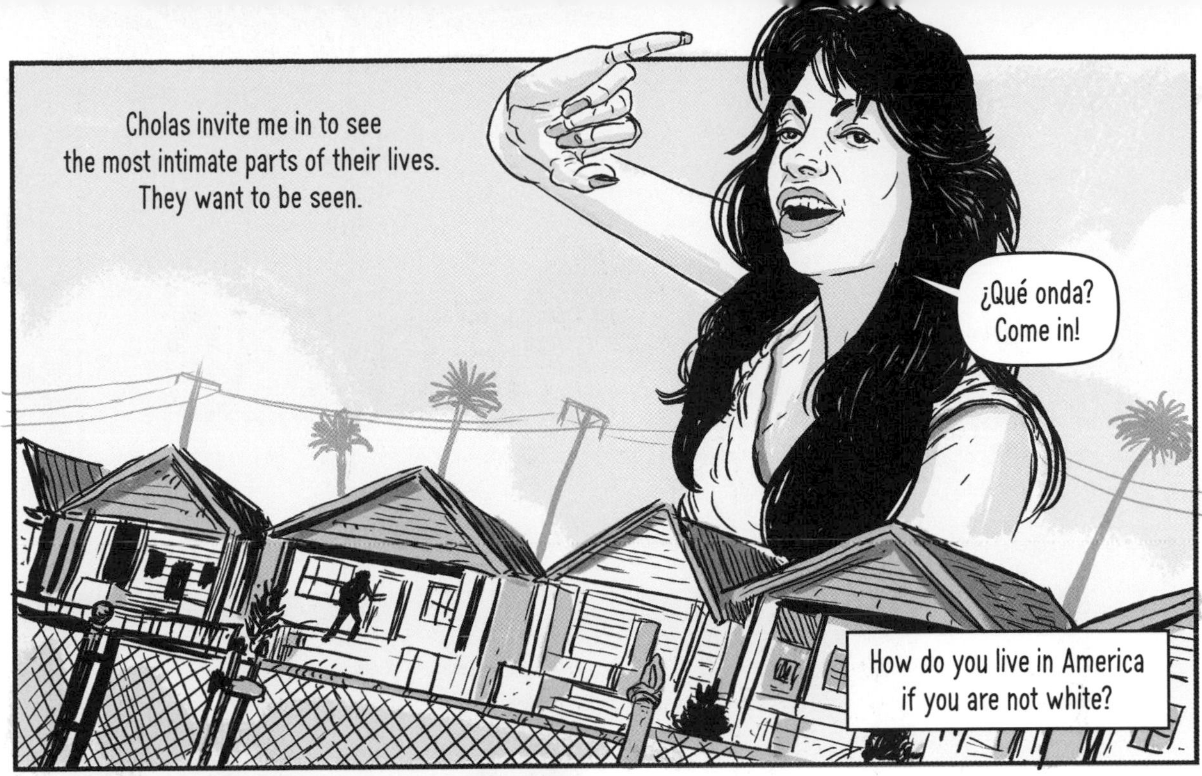
Cholas invite me in to see
the most intimate parts of their lives.
They want to be seen.
¿Qué onda?
Come in!
How do you live in America
if you are not white?

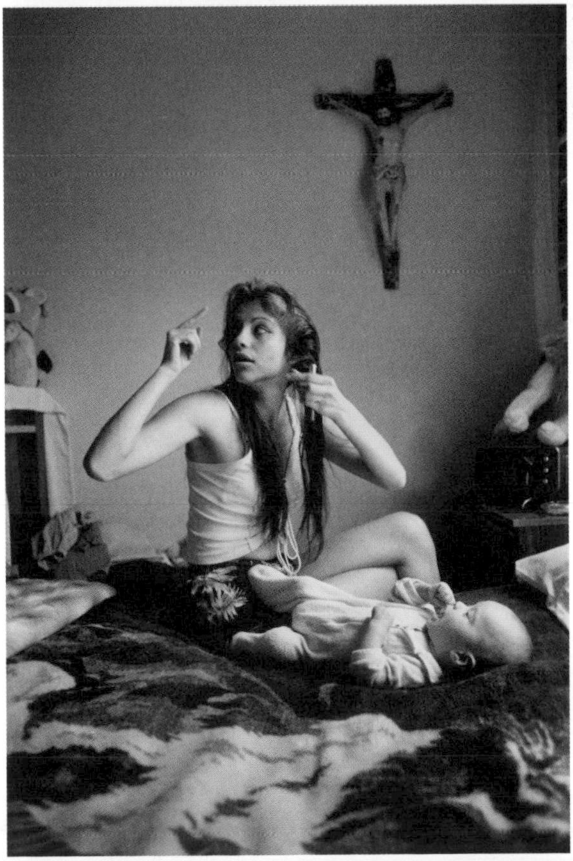

My camera catches glimpses. "American" is a carrot dangled for the people in this house.

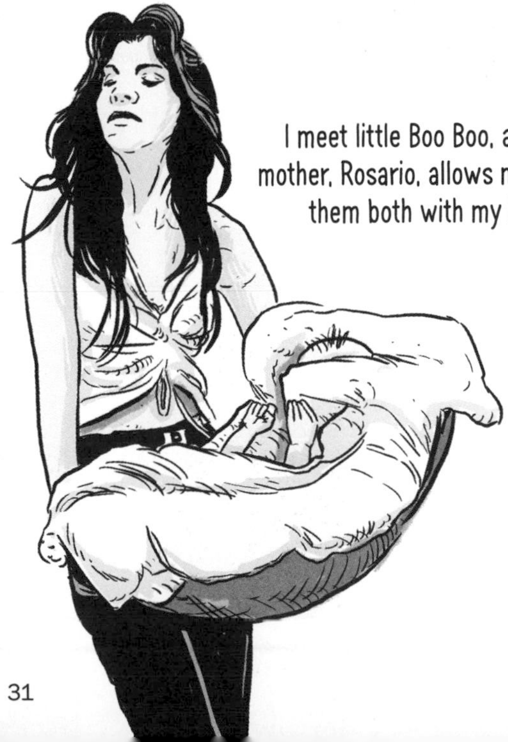

I meet little Boo Boo, and her mother, Rosario, allows me to hold them both with my lens.

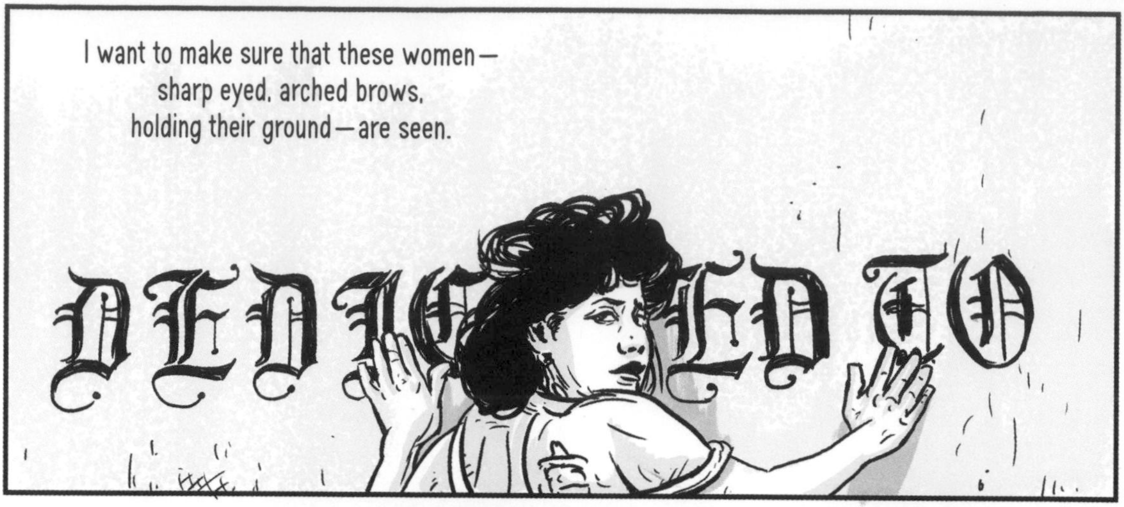
I want to make sure that these women—
sharp eyed, arched brows,
holding their ground—are seen.

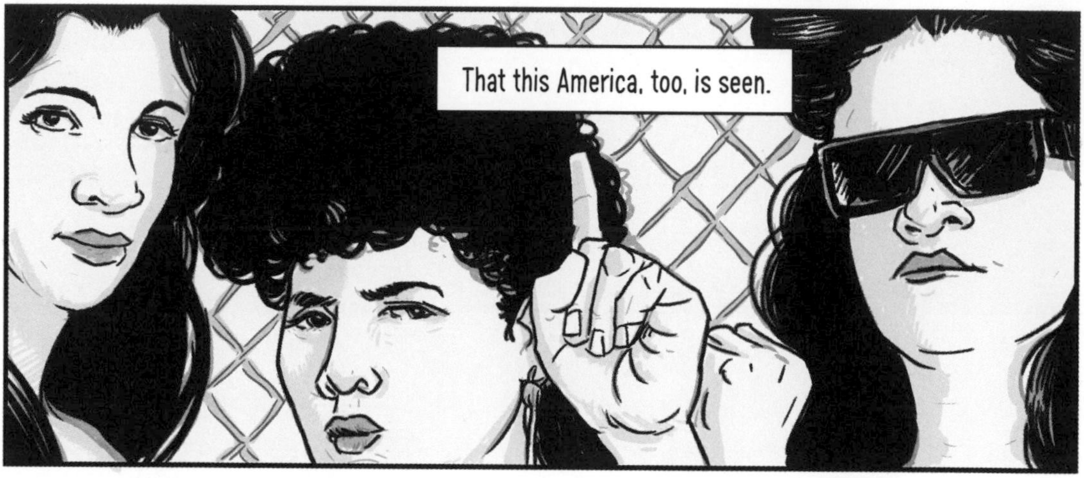
That this America, too, is seen.

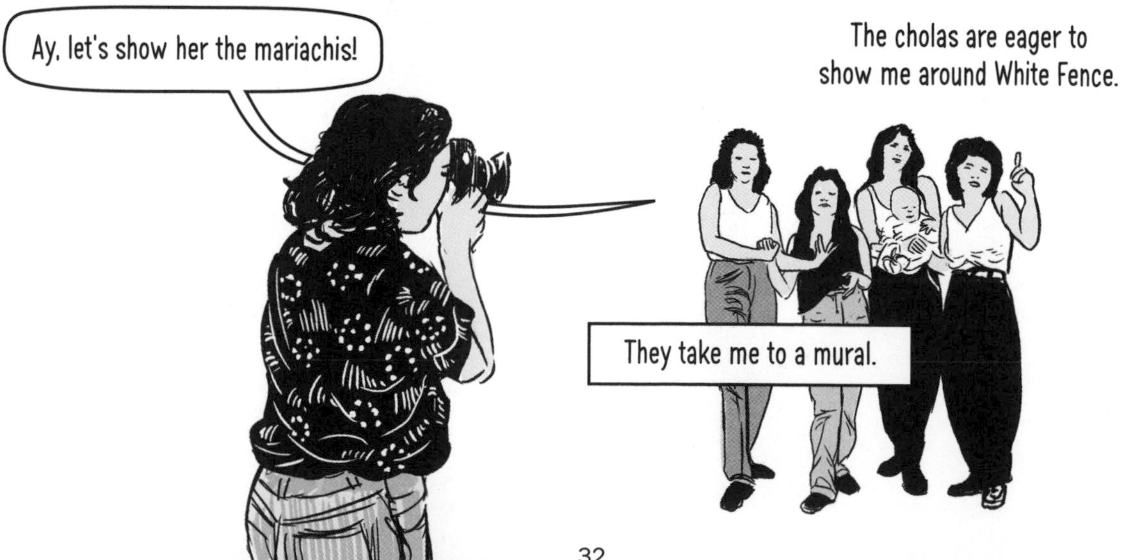
The cholas are eager to show me around White Fence.
Ay, let's show her the mariachis!
They take me to a mural.

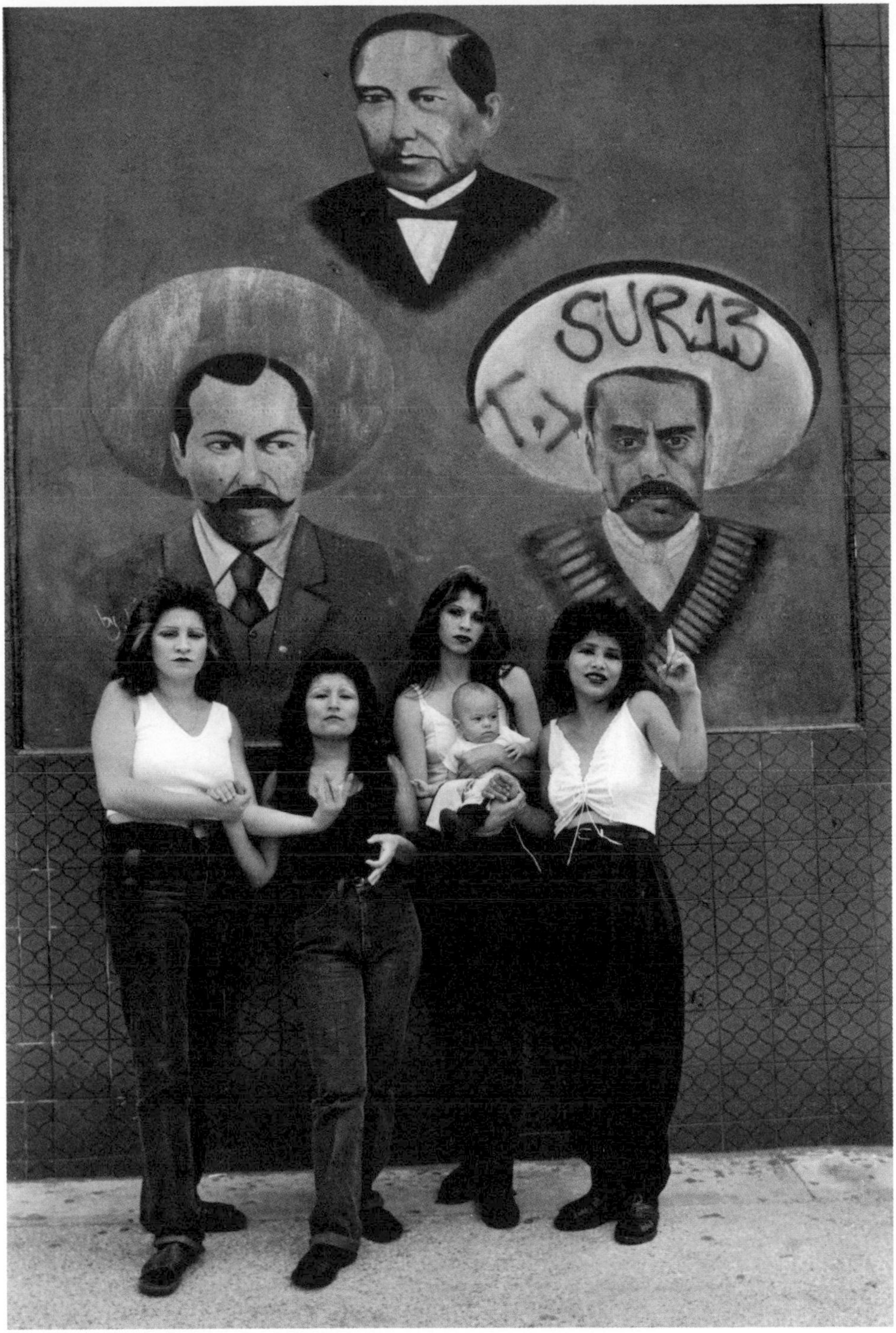
SUR13
T.J

But the mural is not of mariachis. It is of revolutionary Mexicans:
Emiliano Zapata, Benito Juárez, and Pancho Villa.

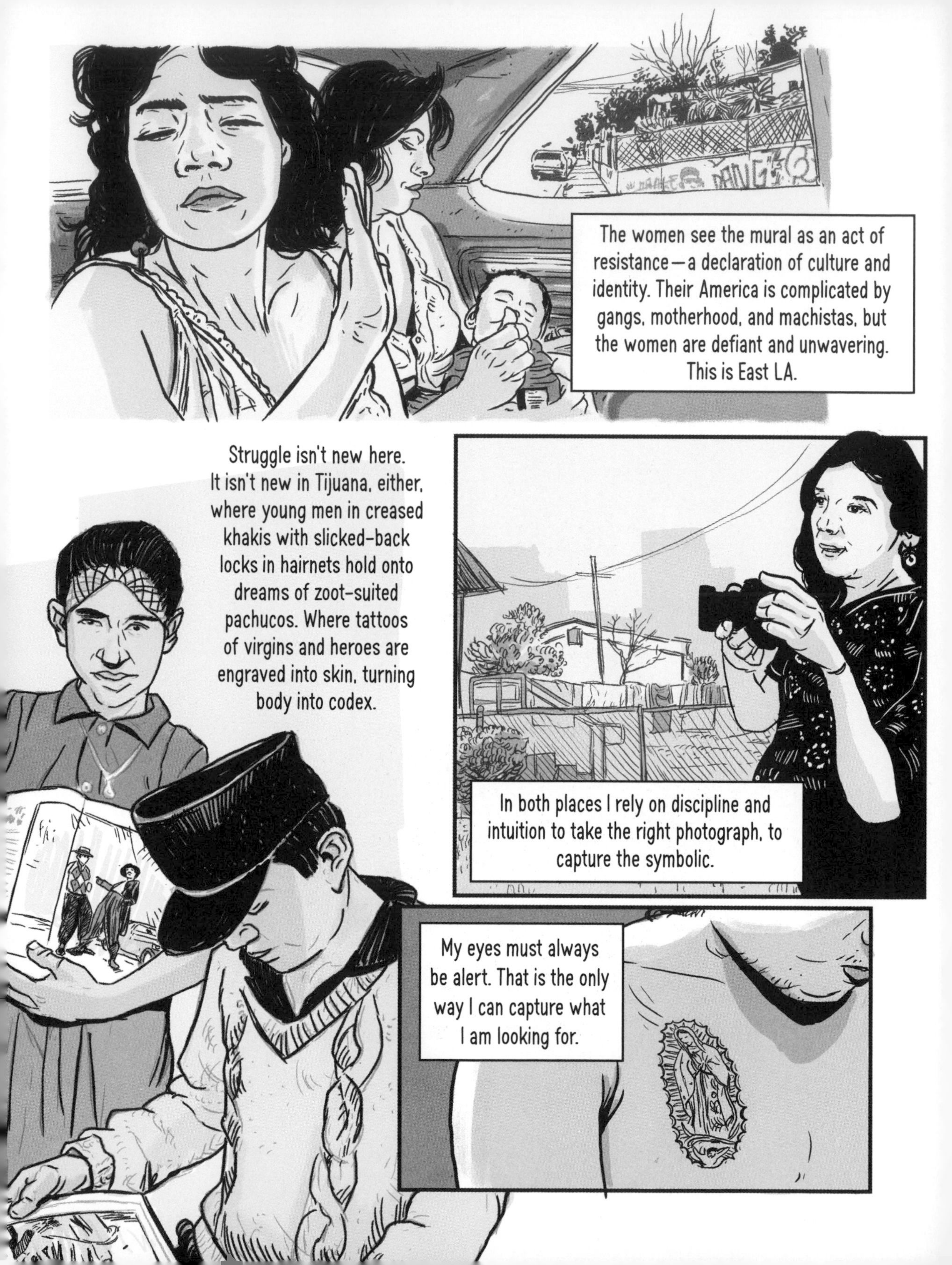

The women see the mural as an act of resistance—a declaration of culture and identity. Their America is complicated by gangs, motherhood, and machistas, but the women are defiant and unwavering. This is East LA.
Struggle isn't new here. It isn't new in Tijuana, either, where young men in creased khakis with slicked-back locks in hairnets hold onto dreams of zoot-suited pachucos. Where tattoos of virgins and heroes are engraved into skin, turning body into codex.
In both places I rely on discipline and intuition to take the right photograph, to capture the symbolic.
My eyes must always be alert. That is the only way I can capture what I am looking for.

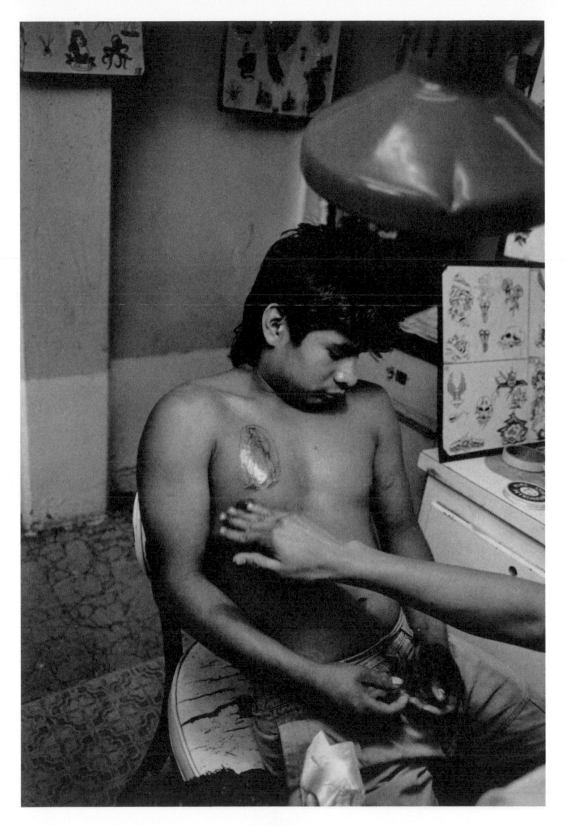

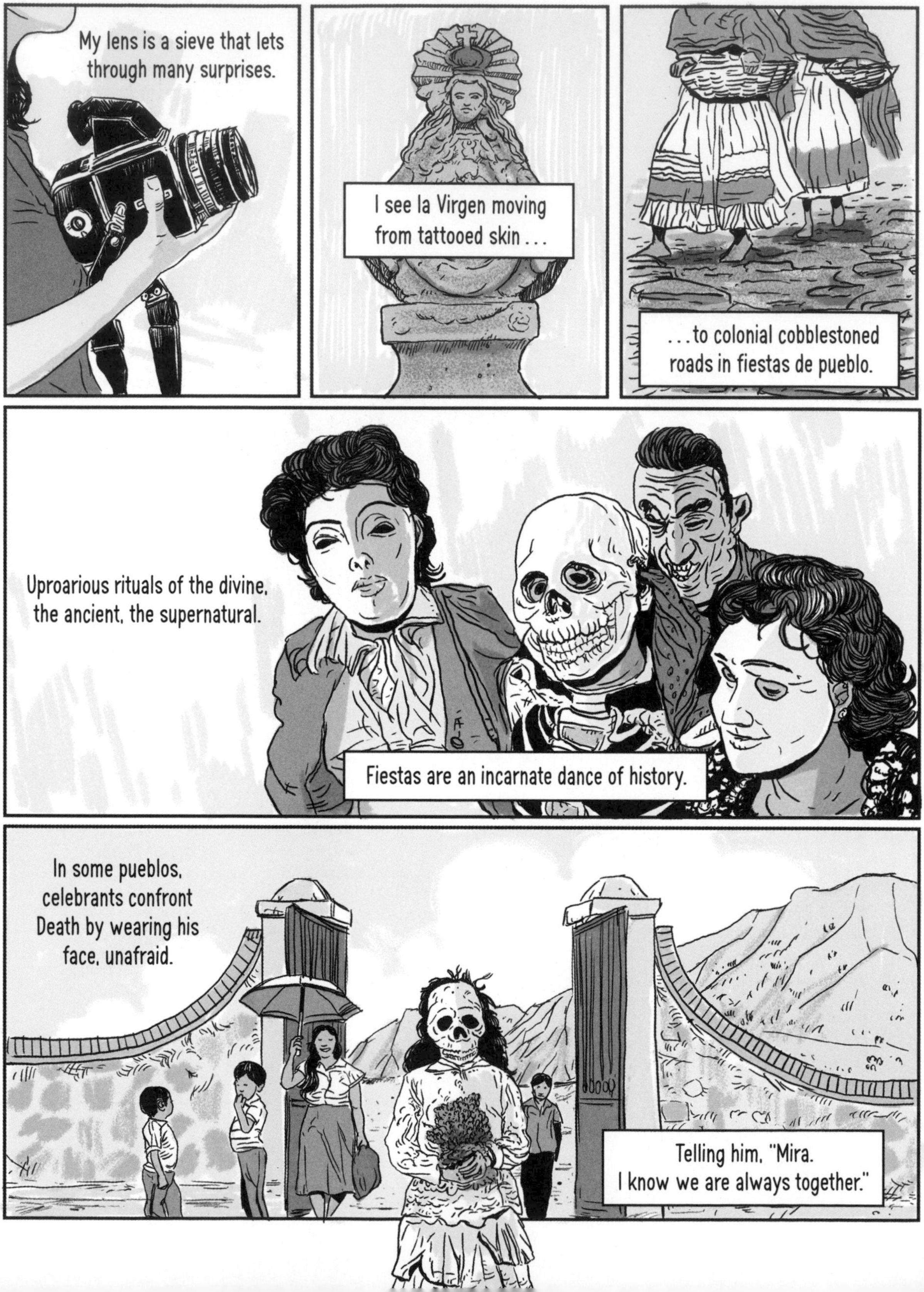
My lens is a sieve that lets through many surprises.
I see la Virgen moving from tattooed skin . . .
. . . to colonial cobblestoned roads in fiestas de pueblo.
Uproarious rituals of the divine, the ancient, the supernatural.
Fiestas are an incarnate dance of history.
In some pueblos, celebrants confront Death by wearing his face, unafraid.
Telling him, "Mira. I know we are always together."

In other pueblos, little girls dressed as la Virgen bring la santísima to life. Everywhere costumes and masks are an essential part of these rituals, pleas, and ecstasies.

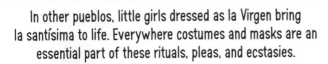

They are passed on from generation to generation.

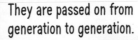

Later, after the film is developed, I study my contact sheets and choose photographs by what surprises me. Some I will never show because I am too disturbed by what they expose.

This is how I get to know my country, how I learn what I'd been missing.

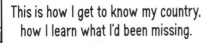

I return to these pueblos several times, taking away something different each visit.

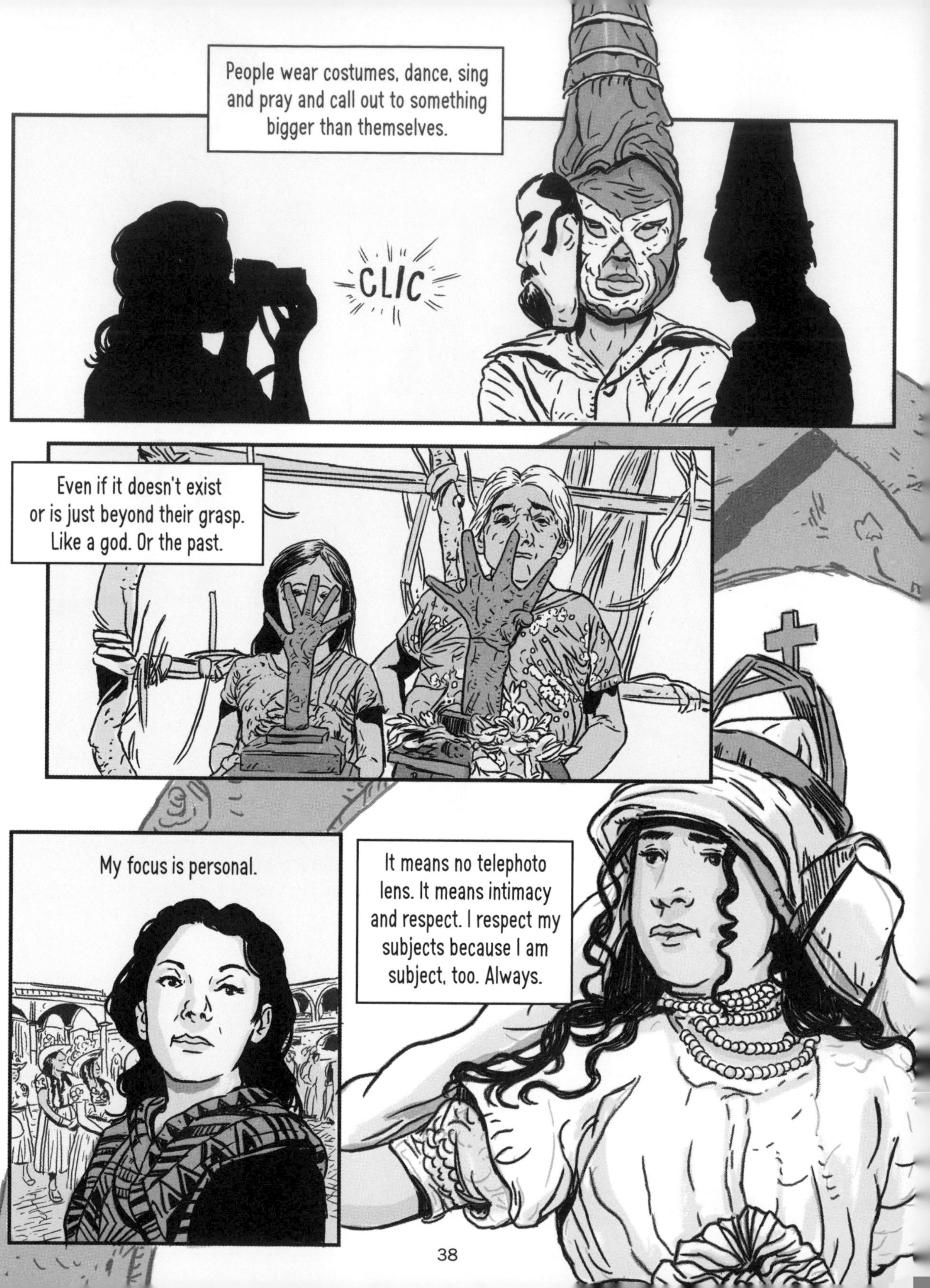
People wear costumes, dance, sing and pray and call out to something bigger than themselves.
CLIC
Even if it doesn't exist or is just beyond their grasp. Like a god. Or the past.
My focus is personal.
It means no telephoto lens. It means intimacy and respect. I respect my subjects because I am subject, too. Always.

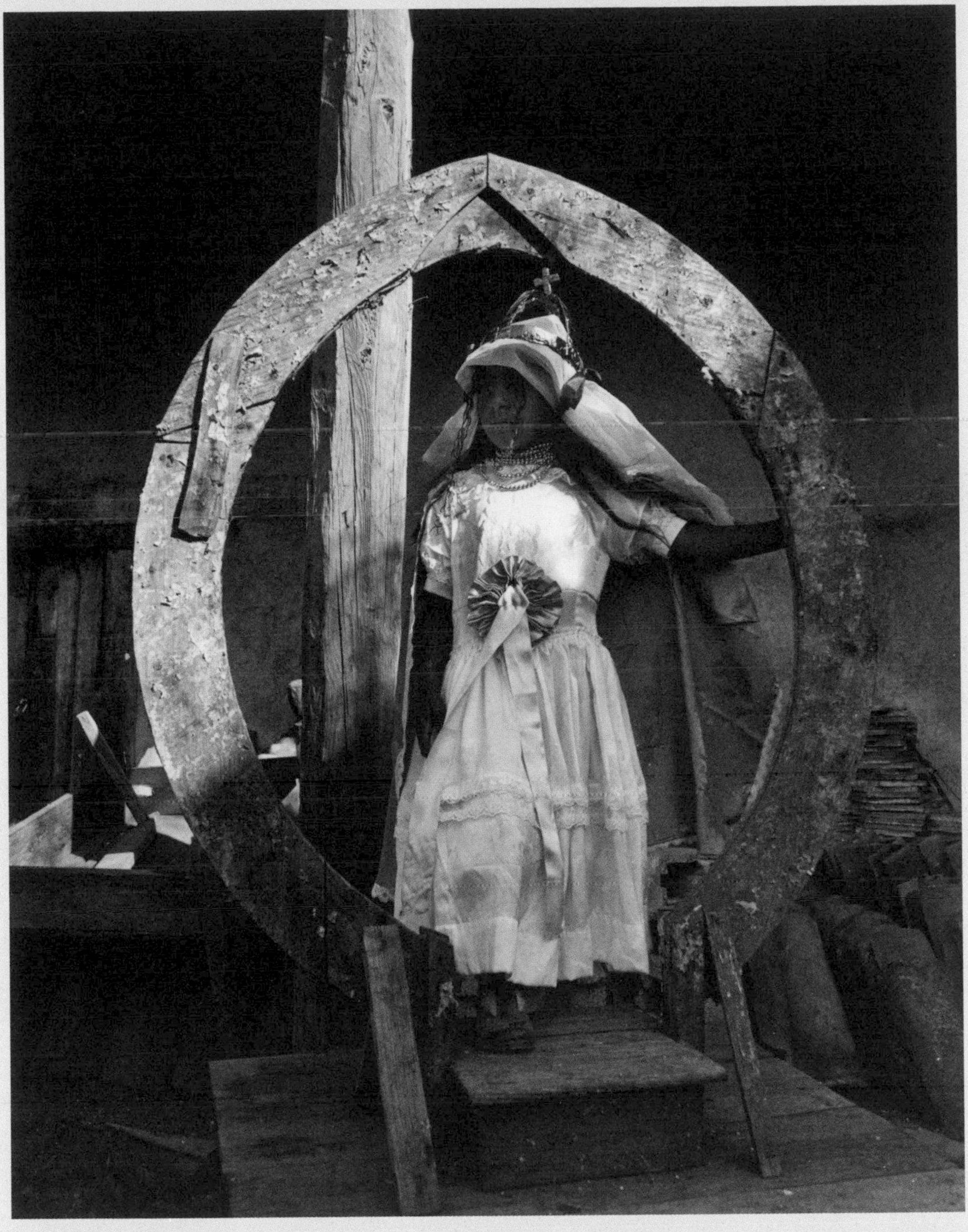

The pueblos I visit become a part of me.
The rituals and symbols show me parts of myself I didn't know were there.
Some of them are serene. Effervescent almost.

Some of them are not. Some of them require blood.

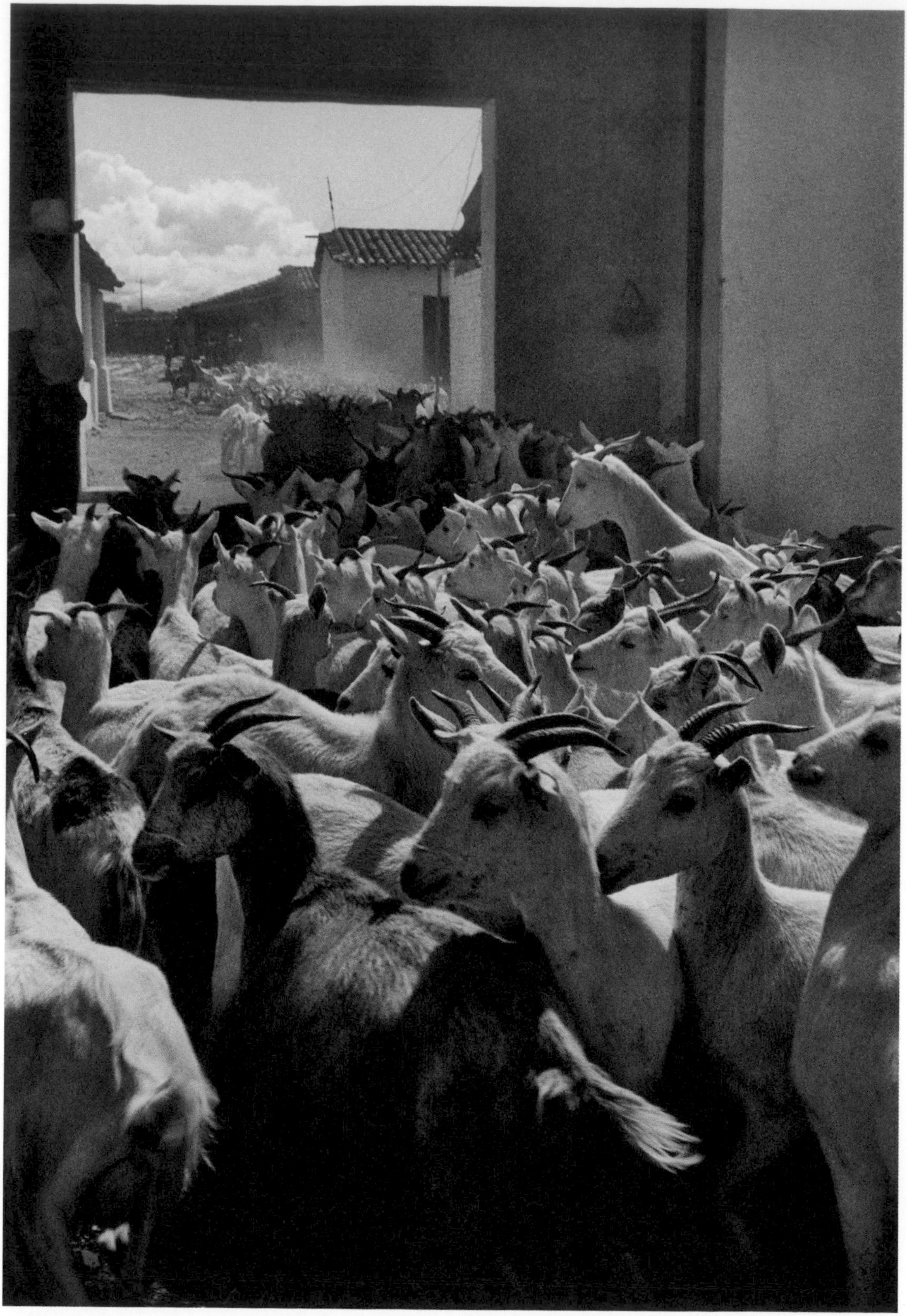

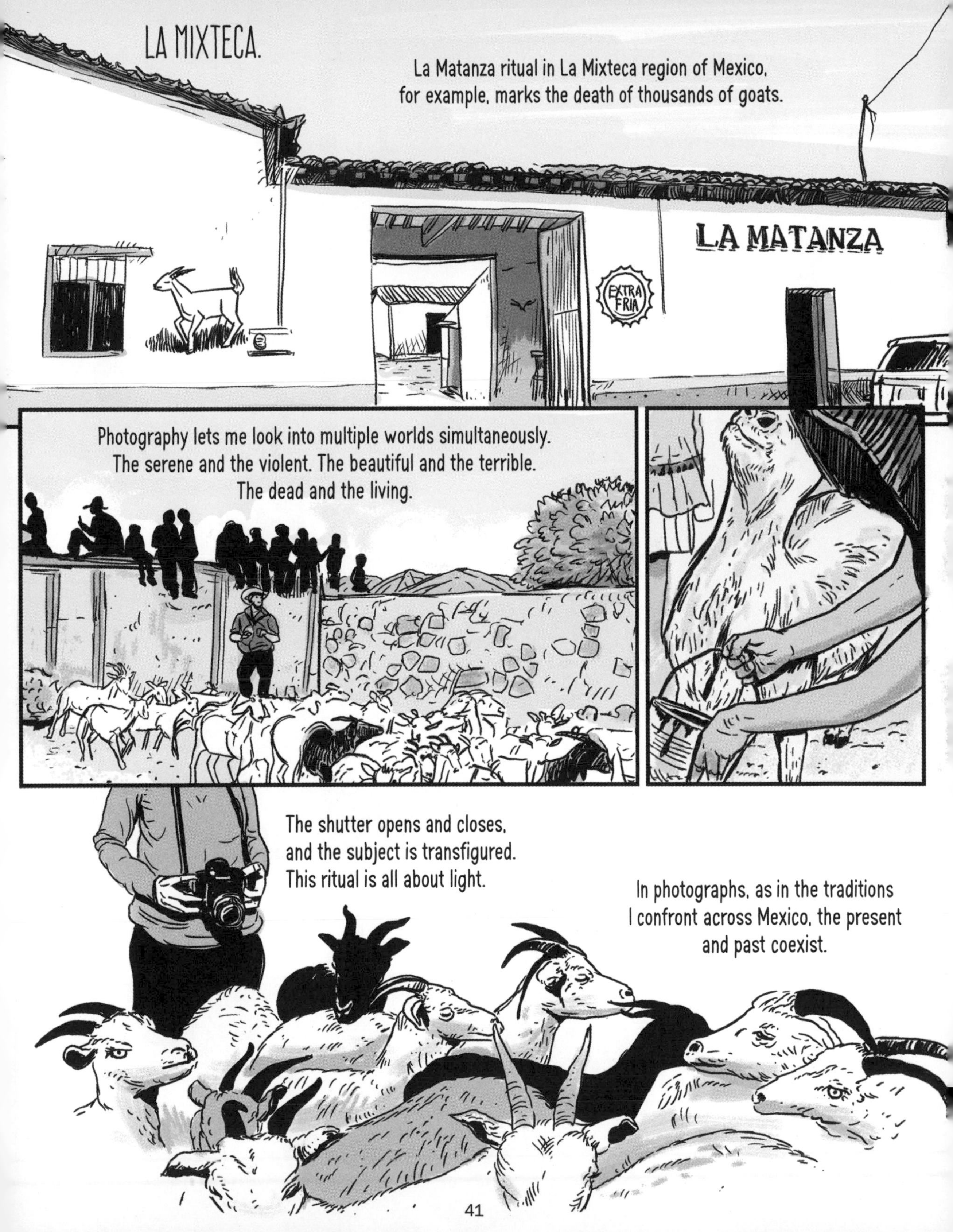
LA MIXTECA.
La Matanza ritual in La Mixteca region of Mexico, for example, marks the death of thousands of goats.
LA MATANZA
EXTRA FRIA
Photography lets me look into multiple worlds simultaneously. The serene and the violent. The beautiful and the terrible. The dead and the living.
The shutter opens and closes, and the subject is transfigured. This ritual is all about light.
In photographs, as in the traditions I confront across Mexico, the present and past coexist.

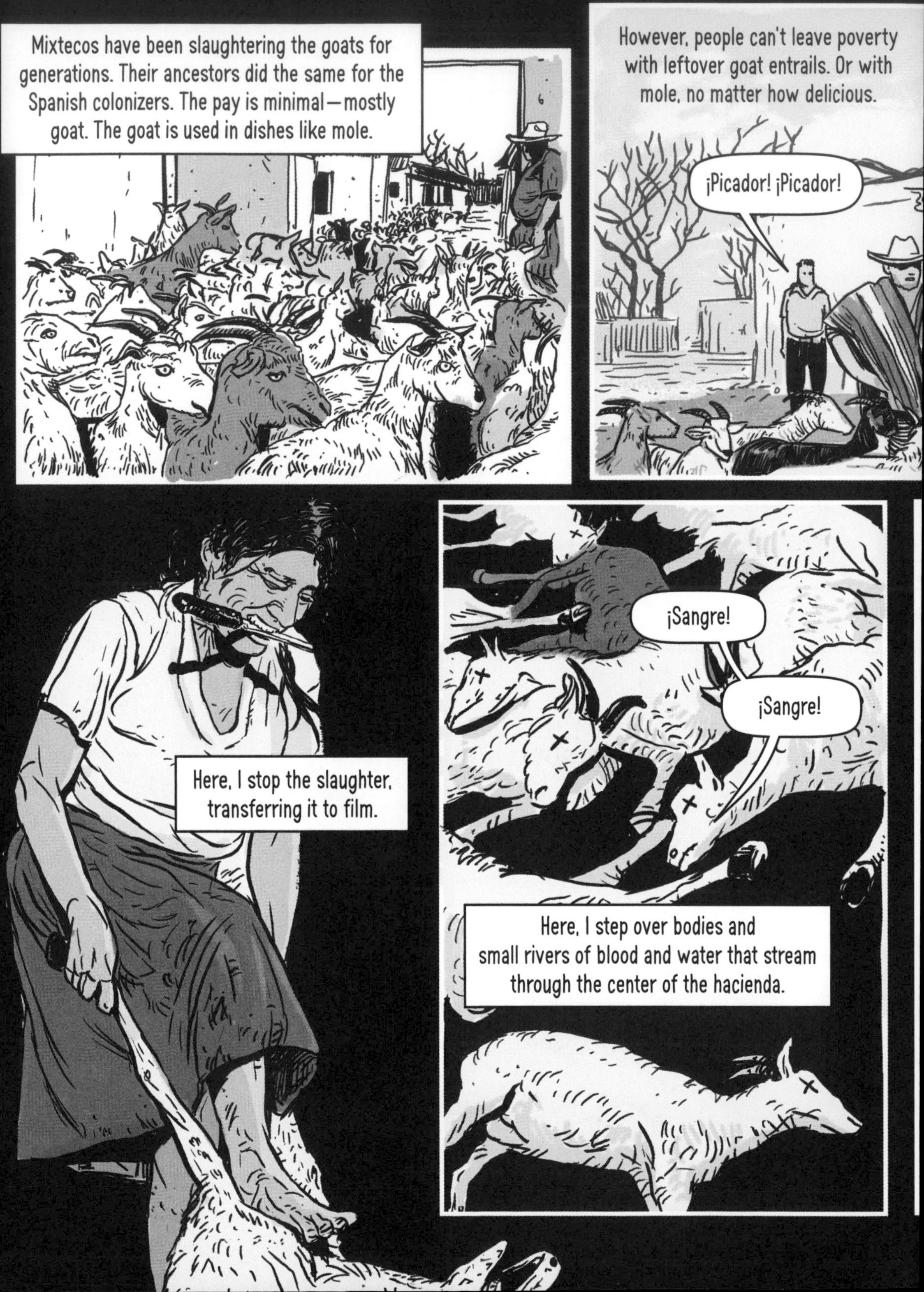
Mixtecos have been slaughtering the goats for generations. Their ancestors did the same for the Spanish colonizers. The pay is minimal—mostly goat. The goat is used in dishes like mole.
However, people can't leave poverty with leftover goat entrails. Or with mole, no matter how delicious.
¡Picador! ¡Picador!
Here, I stop the slaughter, transferring it to film.
¡Sangre!
¡Sangre!
Here, I step over bodies and small rivers of blood and water that stream through the center of the hacienda.

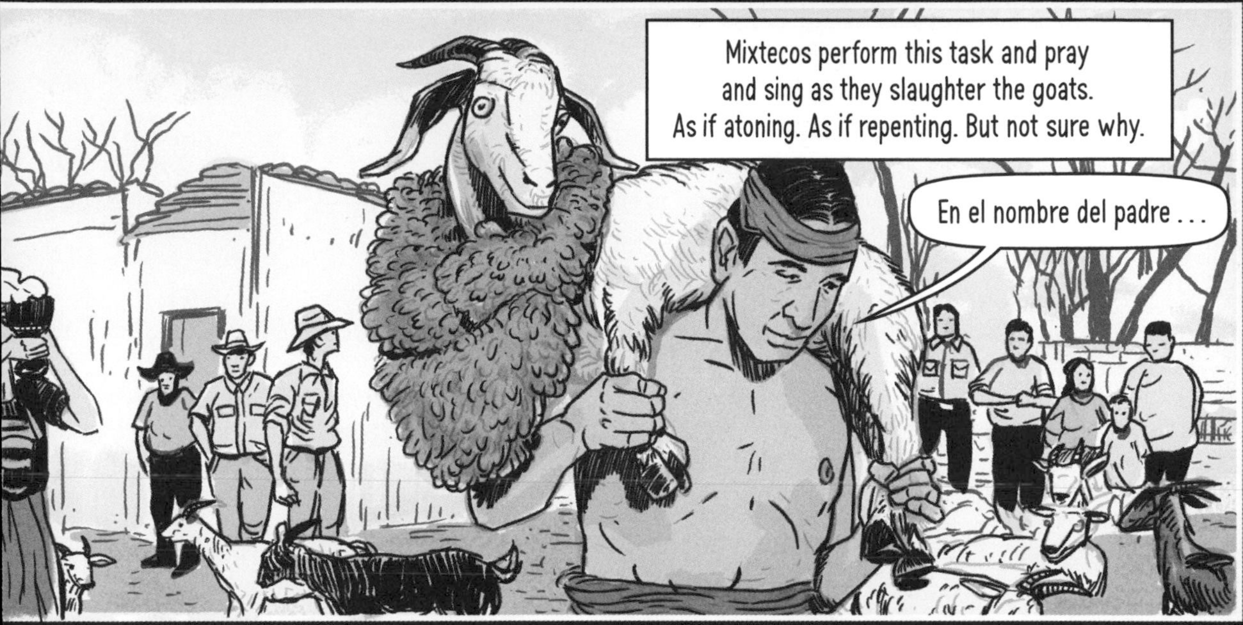
Mixtecos perform this task and pray
and sing as they slaughter the goats.
As if atoning. As if repenting. But not sure why.
En el nombre del padre . . .

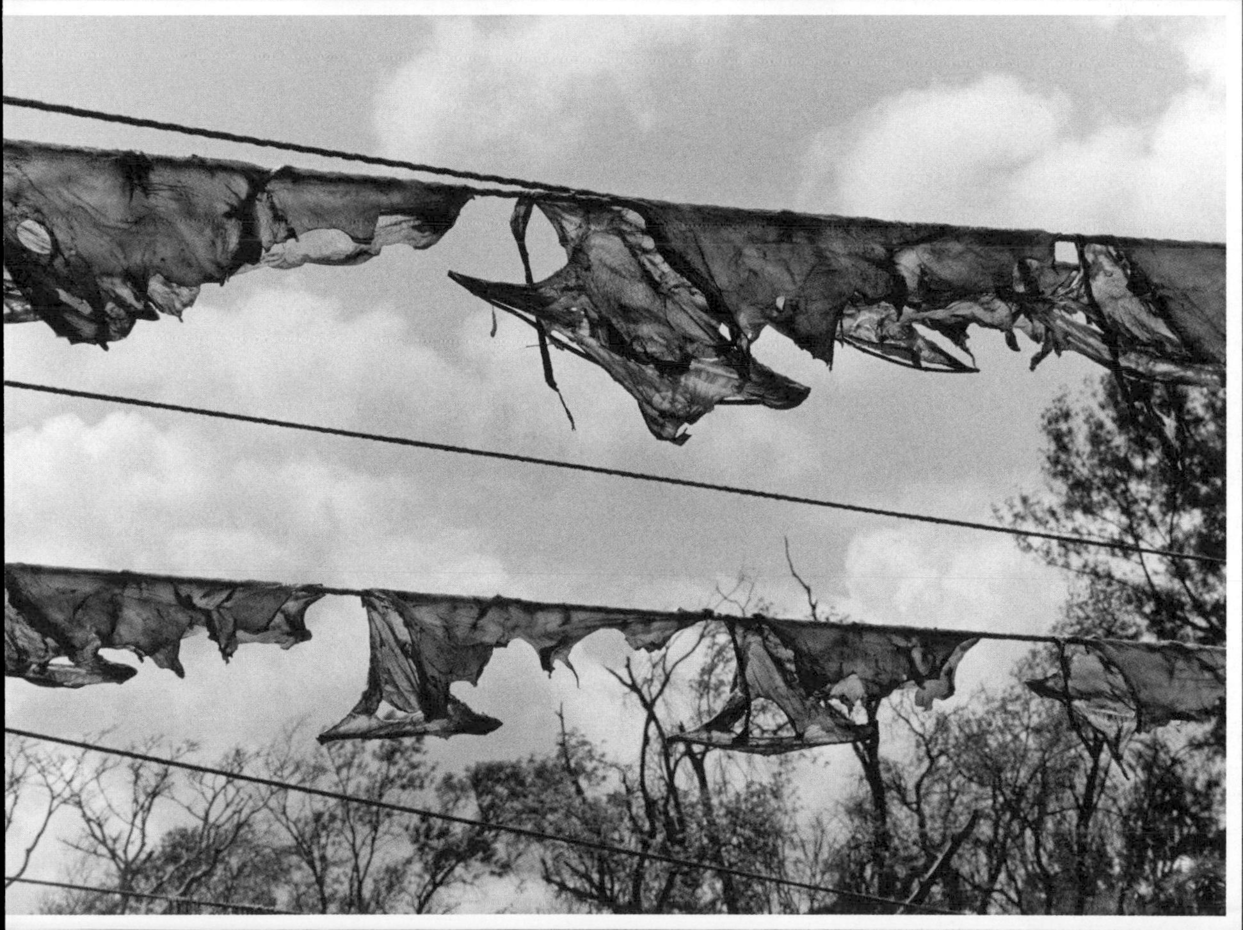

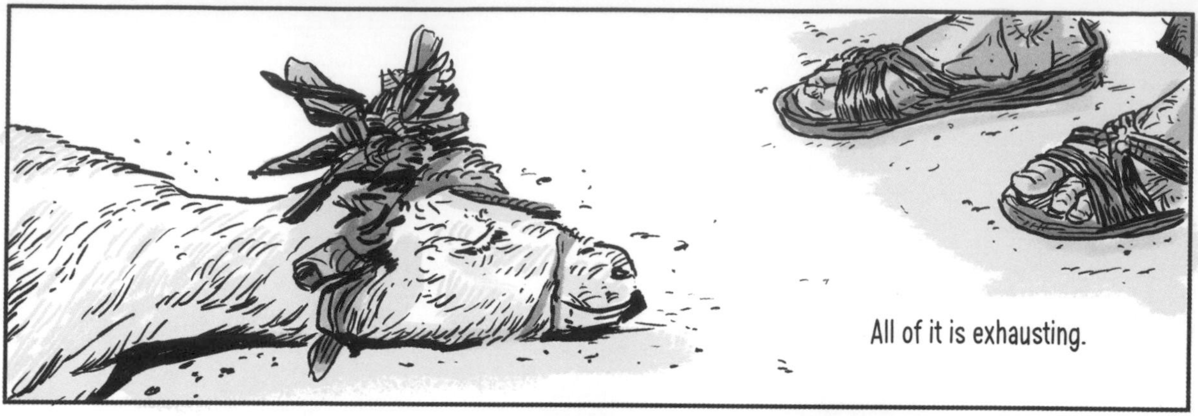
All of it is exhausting.

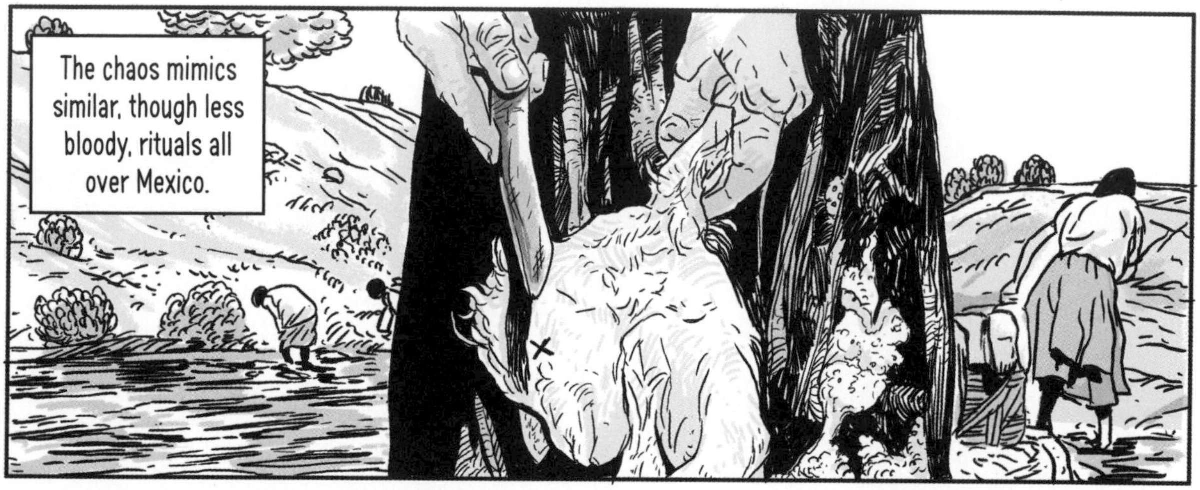
The chaos mimics similar, though less bloody, rituals all over Mexico.

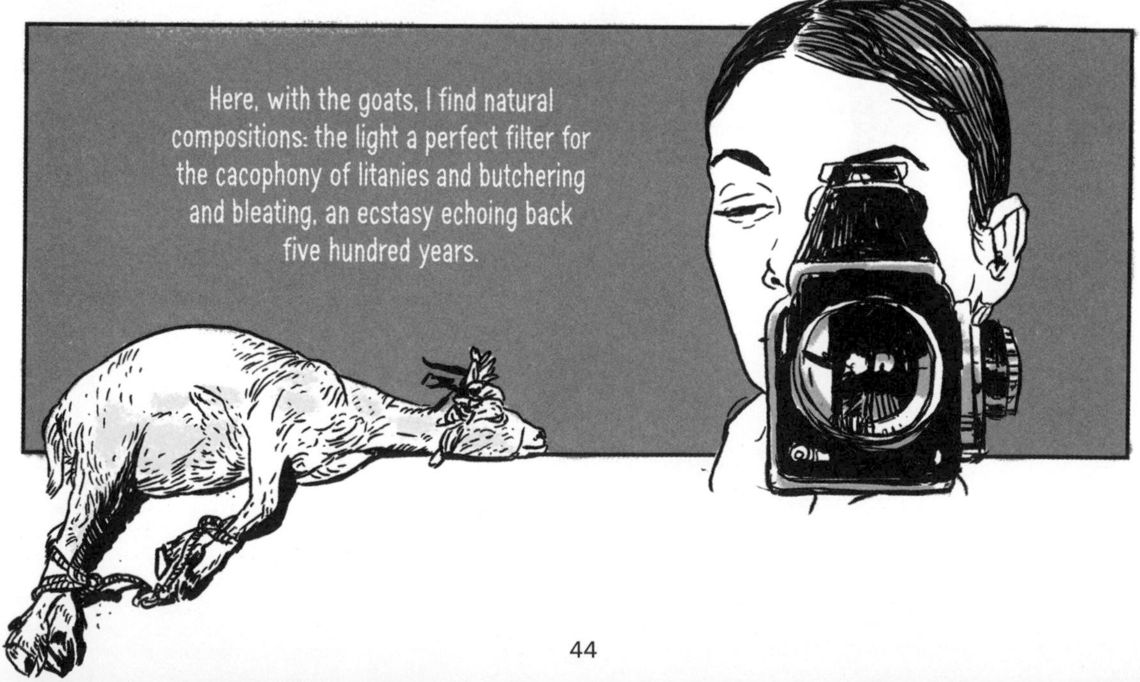
Here, with the goats, I find natural compositions: the light a perfect filter for the cacophony of litanies and butchering and bleating, an ecstasy echoing back five hundred years.

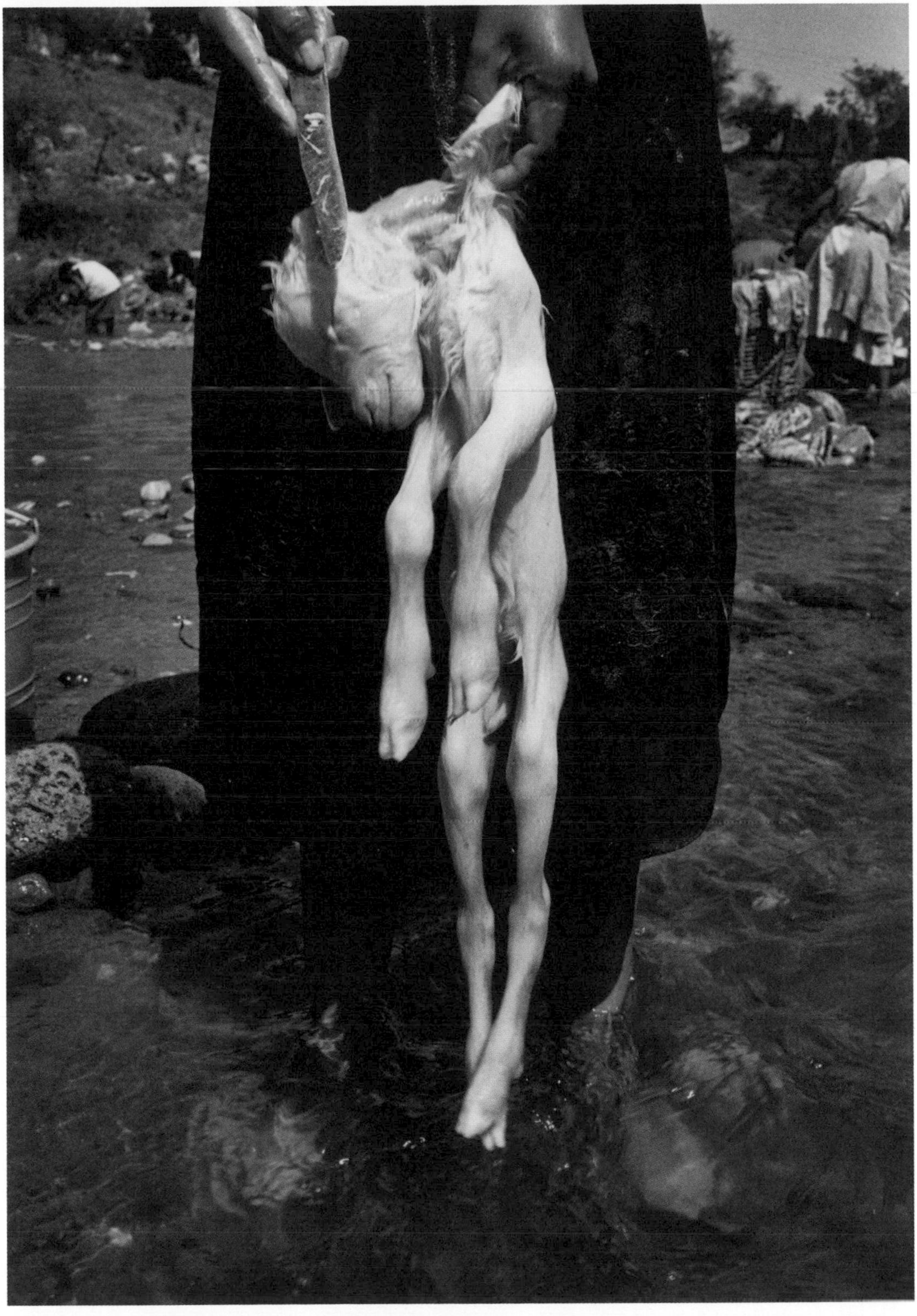

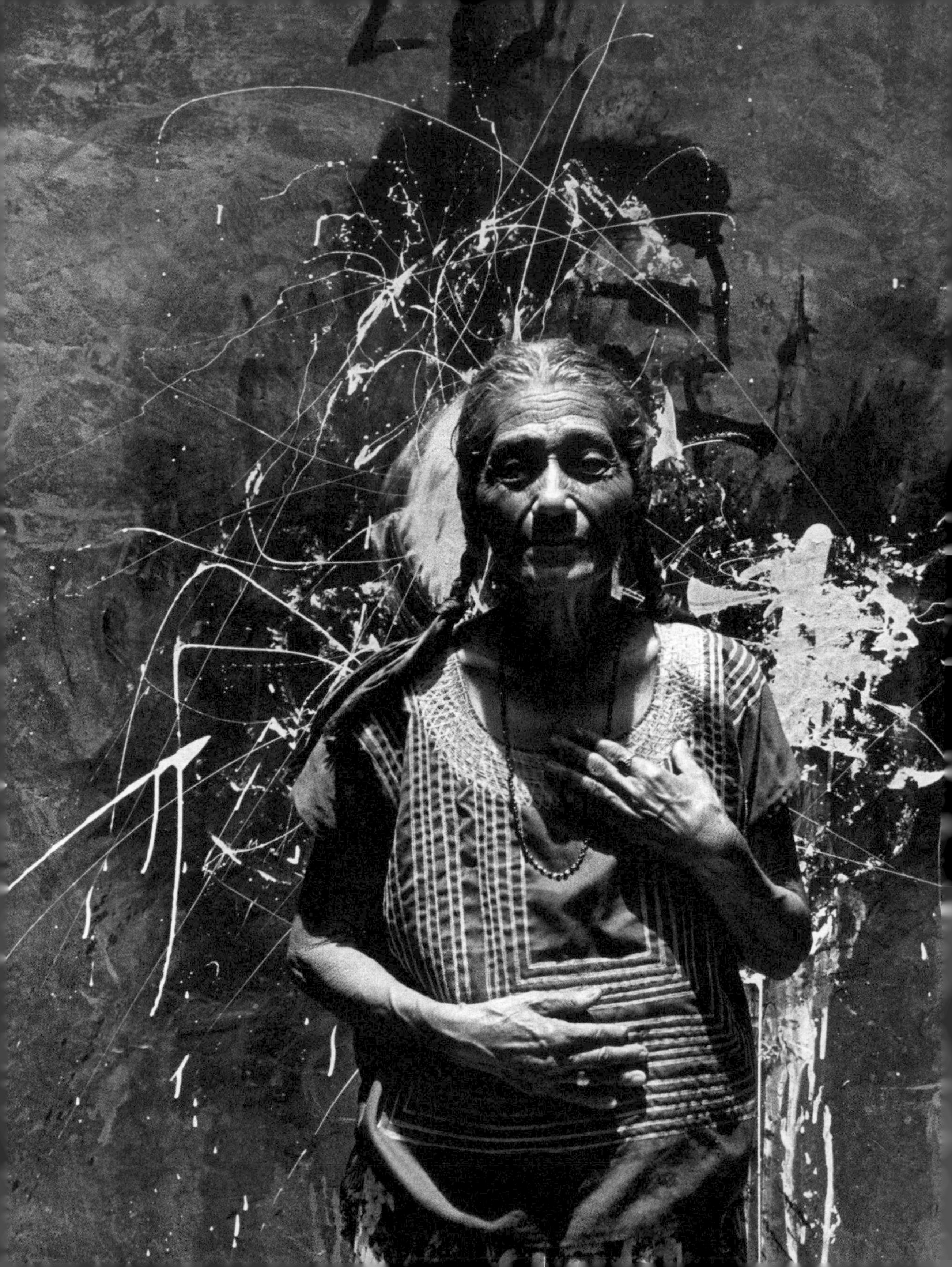

FROM La Mixteca to Juchitán. Juchitán de las mujeres. Juchitán de la mitología. Juchitán, Juchitán, Juchitán. This legendary place exists on the Isthmus of Tehuantepec, in the Mexican state of Oaxaca. It is nothing like the conservative home that Graciela left. The women here do not shy from speaking their minds. But do not confuse this with a matriarchy, Reader. Juchitán is much more complex than what that one word suggests. Juchitán is a place where Zapotec and Spanish conflate. Where gender is not binary.

The project lasts about ten years before Graciela's book on Juchitán comes out. The women and muxes of Juchitán become her friends. Remember, everything for Graciela is complicit. She doesn't work alone. In this case, her friend, the celebrated Mexican author Elena Poniatowska, gives the title to Graciela's book: "Juchitán de las Mujeres." Poniatowska writes about the rituals, erotic songs, and politicized women. Strong women. The women Graciela photographs. But how can one book hold all that Graciela learns there? About herself? About being a woman?

It can't.

The project was actually all Toledo's idea.

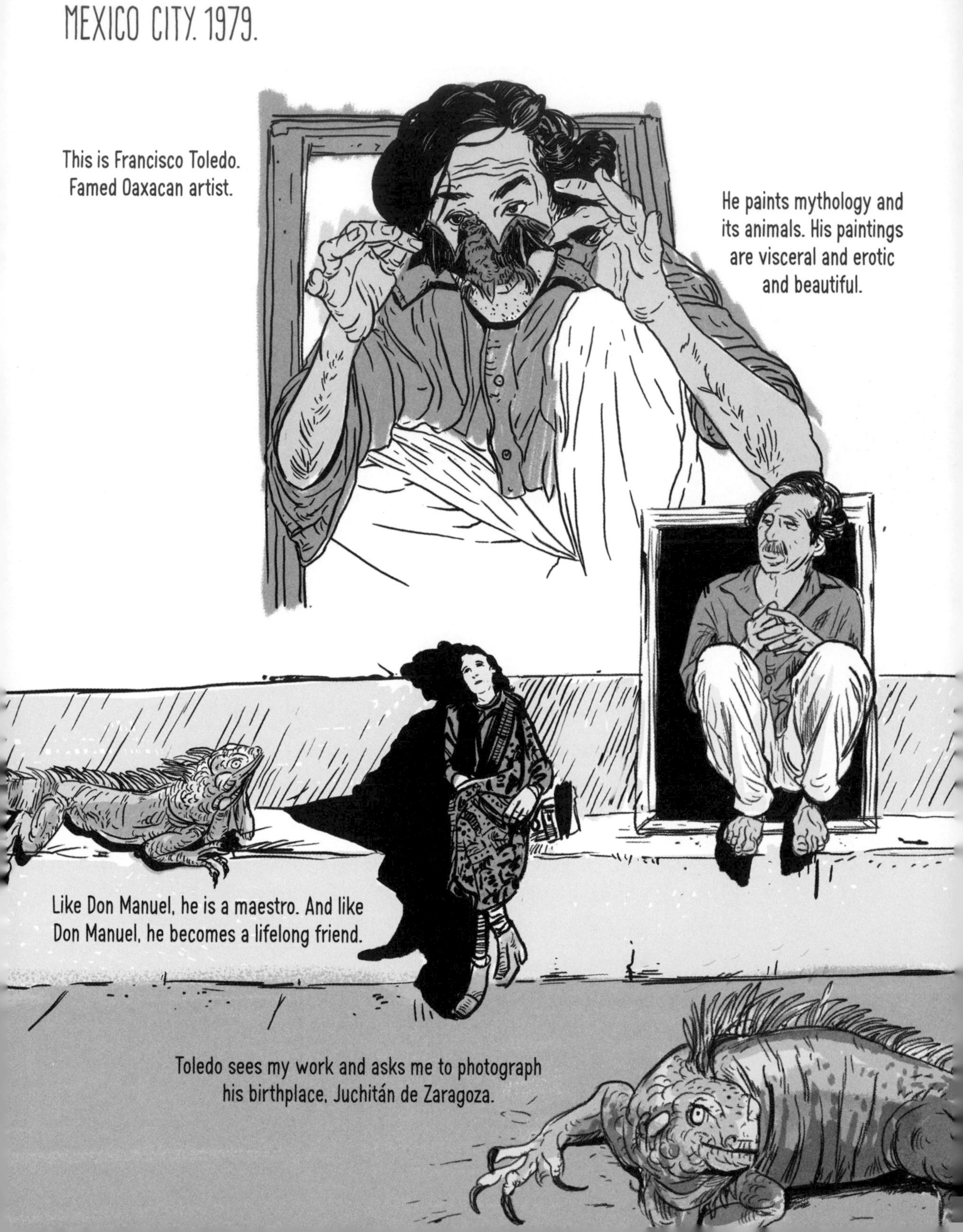
MEXICO CITY. 1979.
This is Francisco Toledo. Famed Oaxacan artist.
He paints mythology and its animals. His paintings are visceral and erotic and beautiful.
Like Don Manuel, he is a maestro. And like Don Manuel, he becomes a lifelong friend.
Toledo sees my work and asks me to photograph his birthplace, Juchitán de Zaragoza.

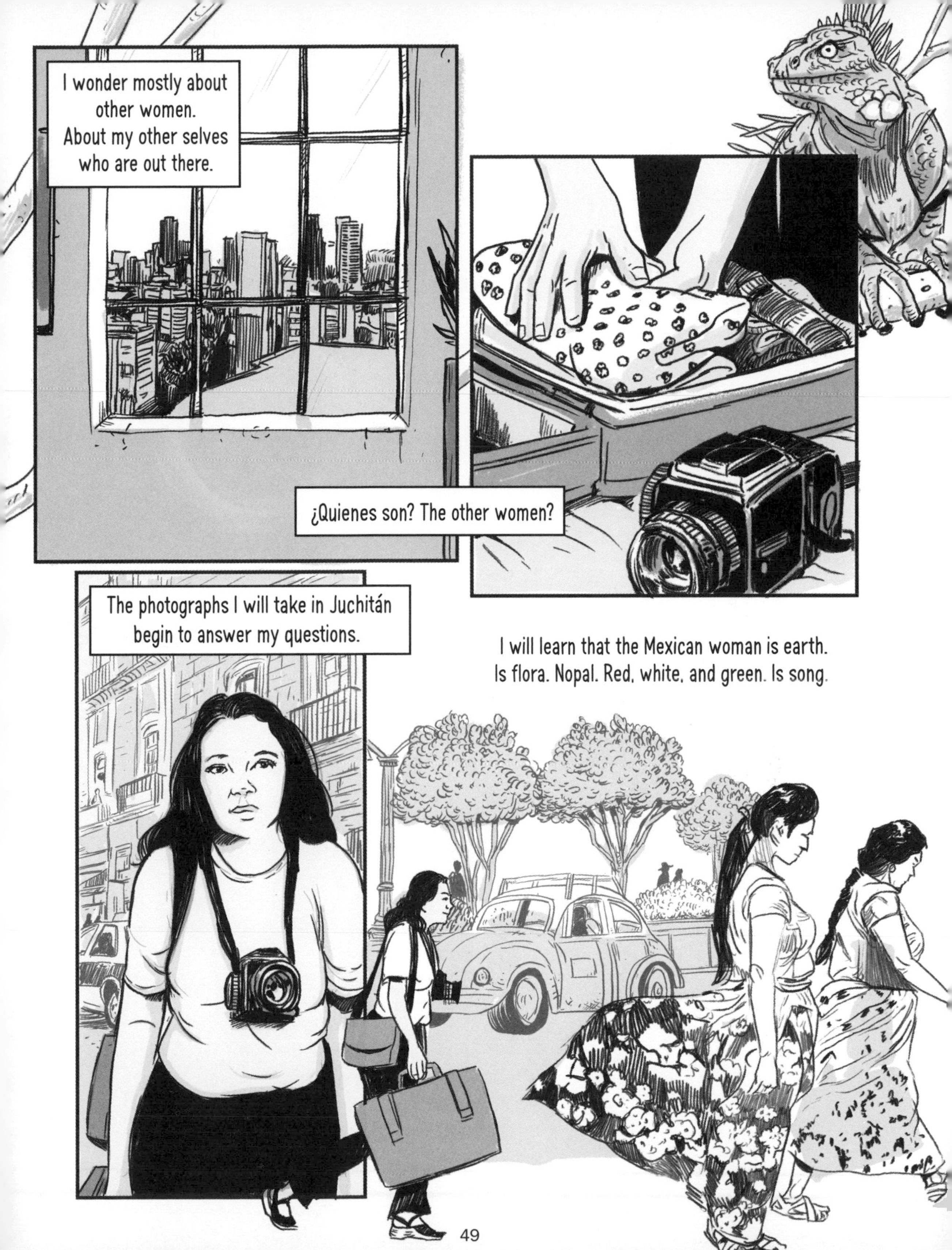
I wonder mostly about other women. About my other selves who are out there.
¿Quienes son? The other women?
The photographs I will take in Juchitán begin to answer my questions.
I will learn that the Mexican woman is earth. Is flora. Nopal. Red, white, and green. Is song.

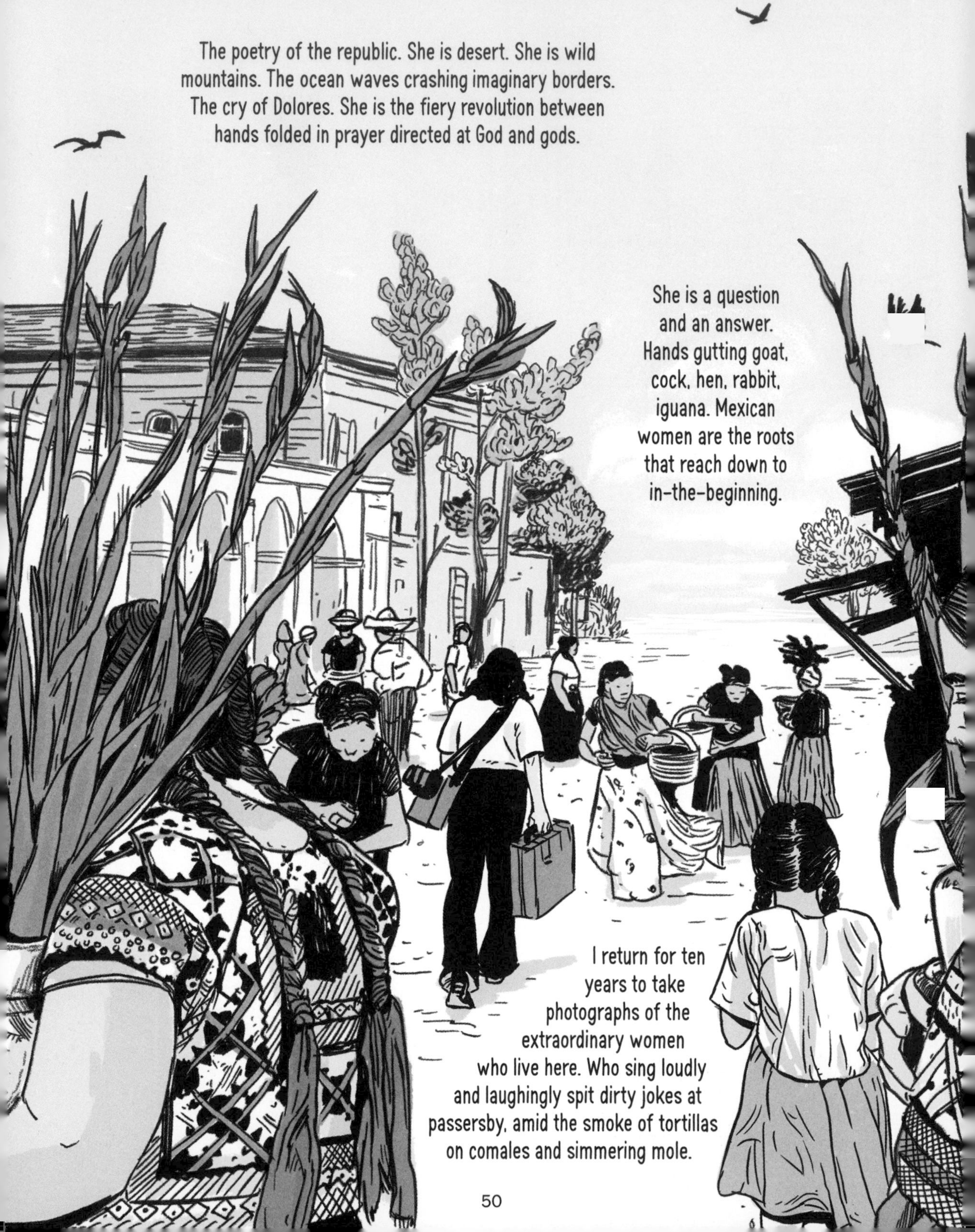
The poetry of the republic. She is desert. She is wild mountains. The ocean waves crashing imaginary borders. The cry of Dolores. She is the fiery revolution between hands folded in prayer directed at God and gods.
She is a question and an answer. Hands gutting goat, cock, hen, rabbit, iguana. Mexican women are the roots that reach down to in-the-beginning.
I return for ten years to take photographs of the extraordinary women who live here. Who sing loudly and laughingly spit dirty jokes at passersby, amid the smoke of tortillas on comales and simmering mole.

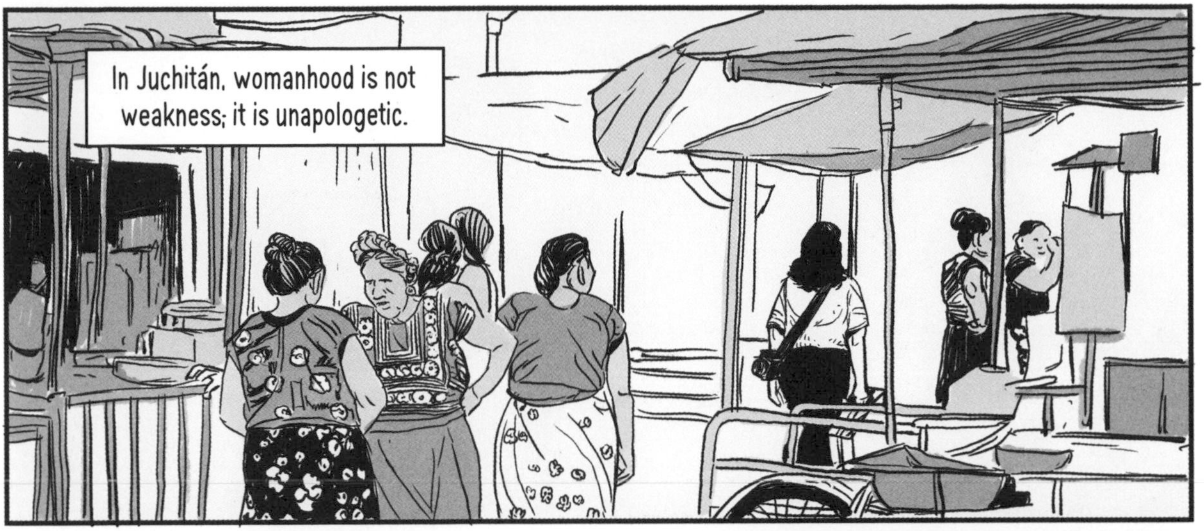
In Juchitán, womanhood is not weakness; it is unapologetic.

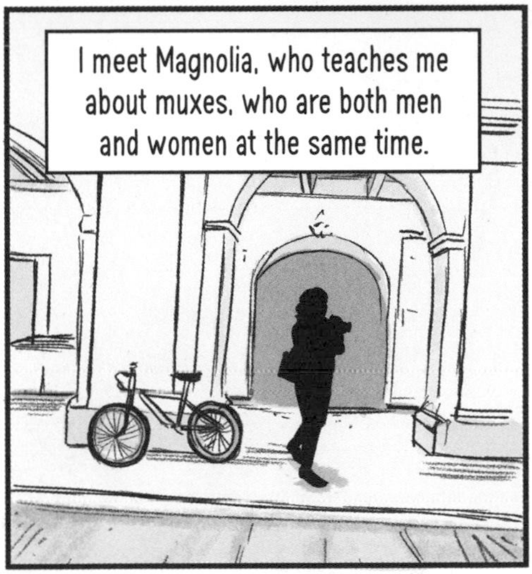
I meet Magnolia, who teaches me about muxes, who are both men and women at the same time.

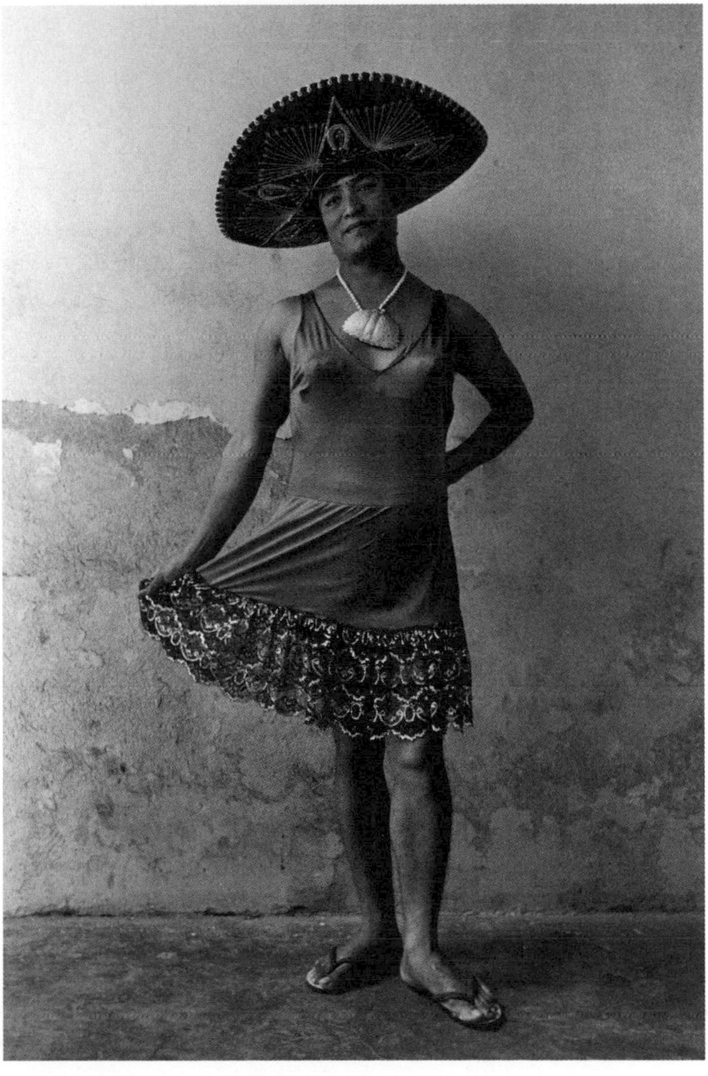

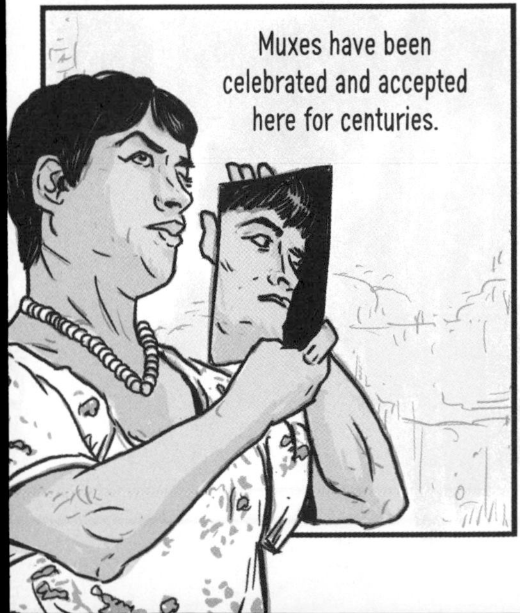
Muxes have been celebrated and accepted here for centuries.

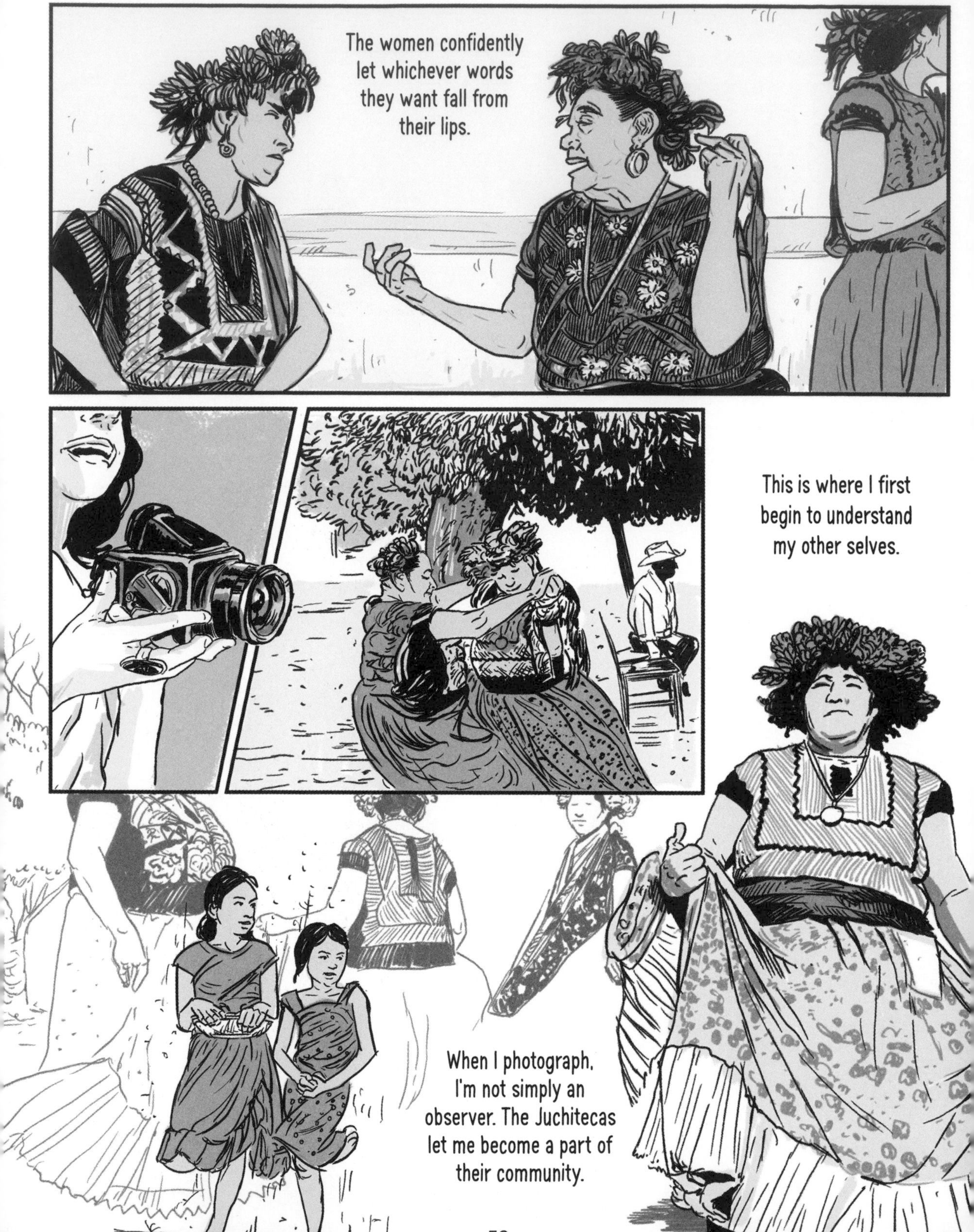
The women confidently let whichever words they want fall from their lips.
This is where I first begin to understand my other selves.
When I photograph, I'm not simply an observer. The Juchitecas let me become a part of their community.

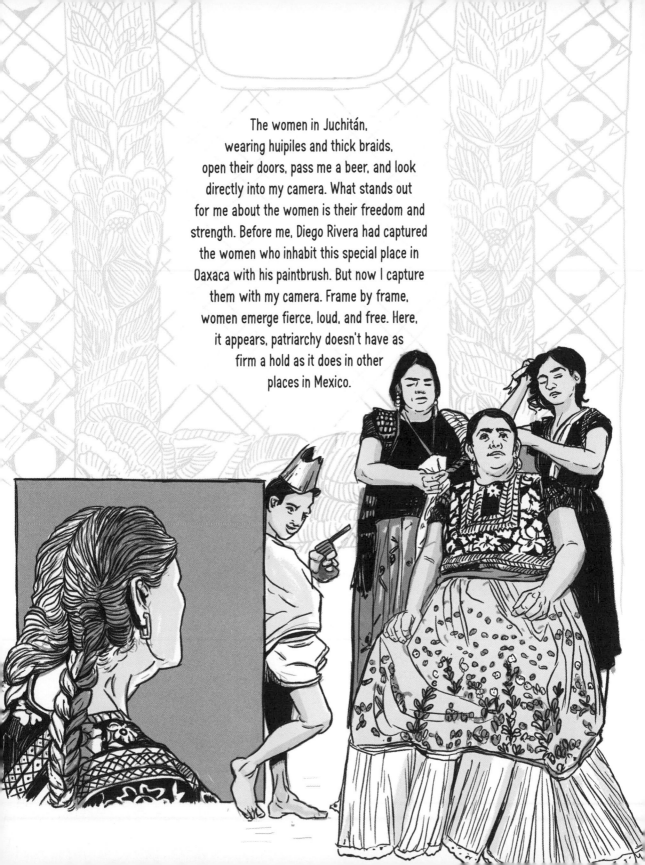

The women in Juchitán,
wearing huipiles and thick braids,
open their doors, pass me a beer, and look
directly into my camera. What stands out
for me about the women is their freedom and
strength. Before me, Diego Rivera had captured
the women who inhabit this special place in
Oaxaca with his paintbrush. But now I capture
them with my camera. Frame by frame,
women emerge fierce, loud, and free. Here,
it appears, patriarchy doesn't have as
firm a hold as it does in other
places in Mexico.

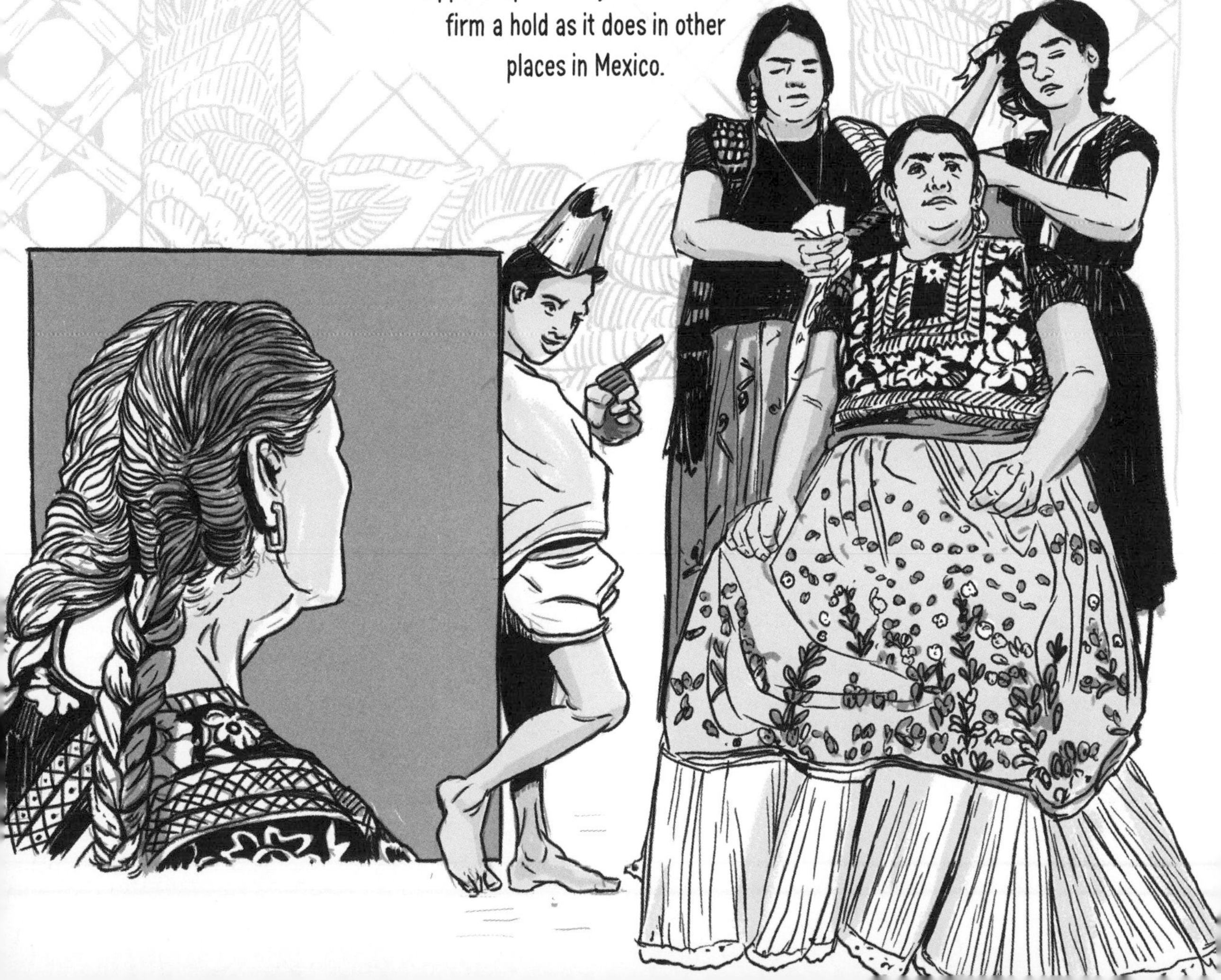

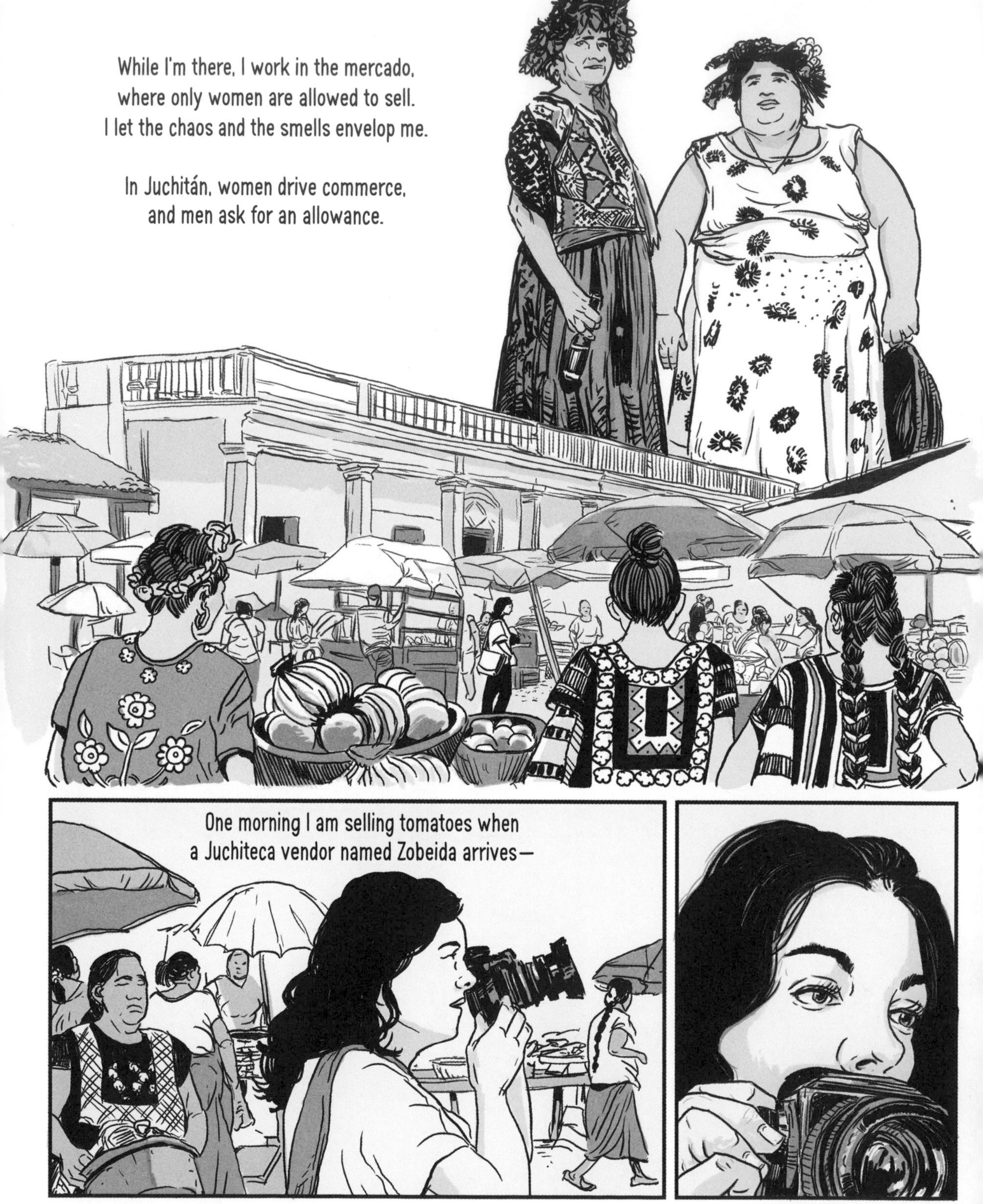
While I'm there, I work in the mercado, where only women are allowed to sell. I let the chaos and the smells envelop me.
In Juchitán, women drive commerce, and men ask for an allowance.
One morning I am selling tomatoes when a Juchiteca vendor named Zobeida arrives—

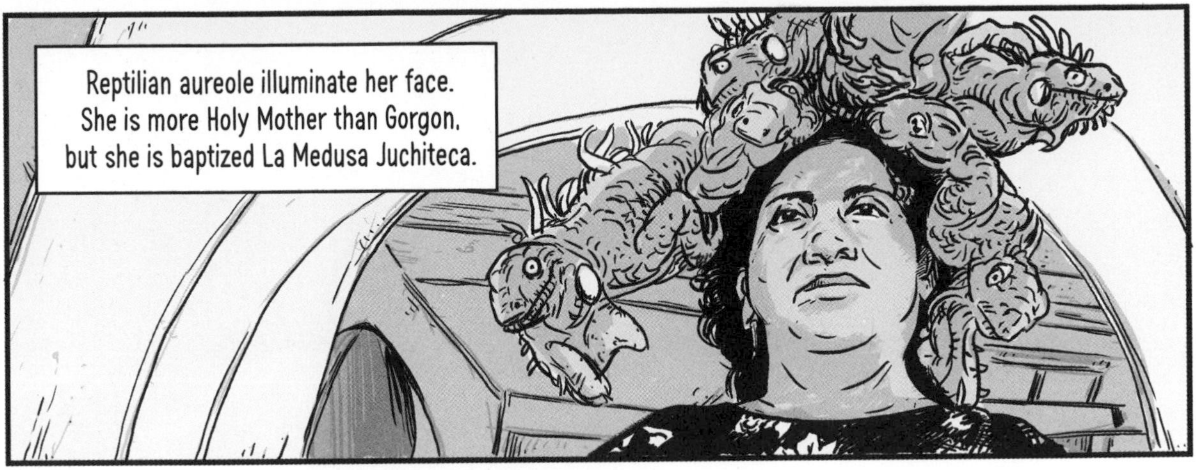
Reptilian aureole illuminate her face.
She is more Holy Mother than Gorgon,
but she is baptized La Medusa Juchiteca.

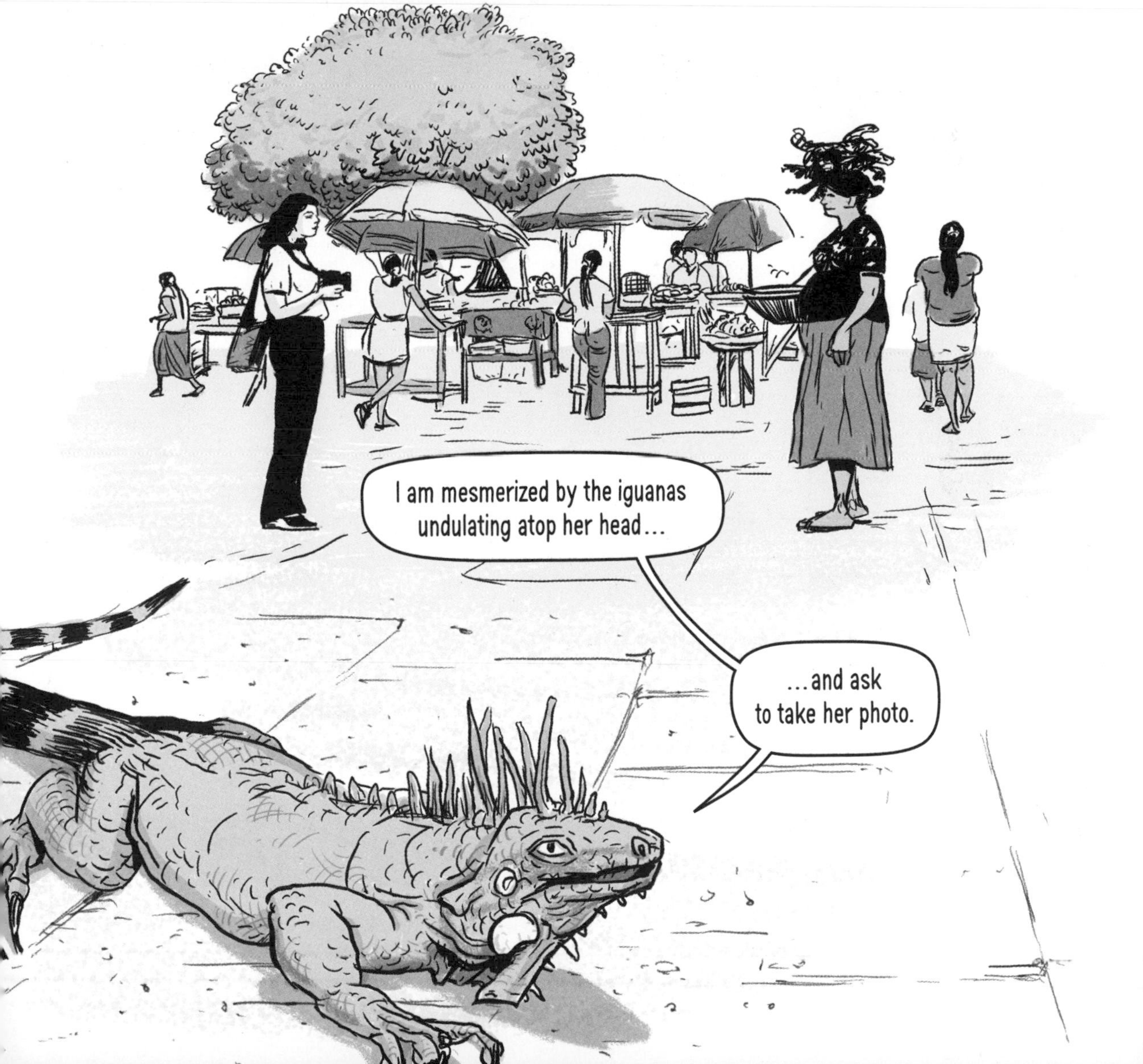
I am mesmerized by the iguanas undulating atop her head...
...and ask to take her photo.

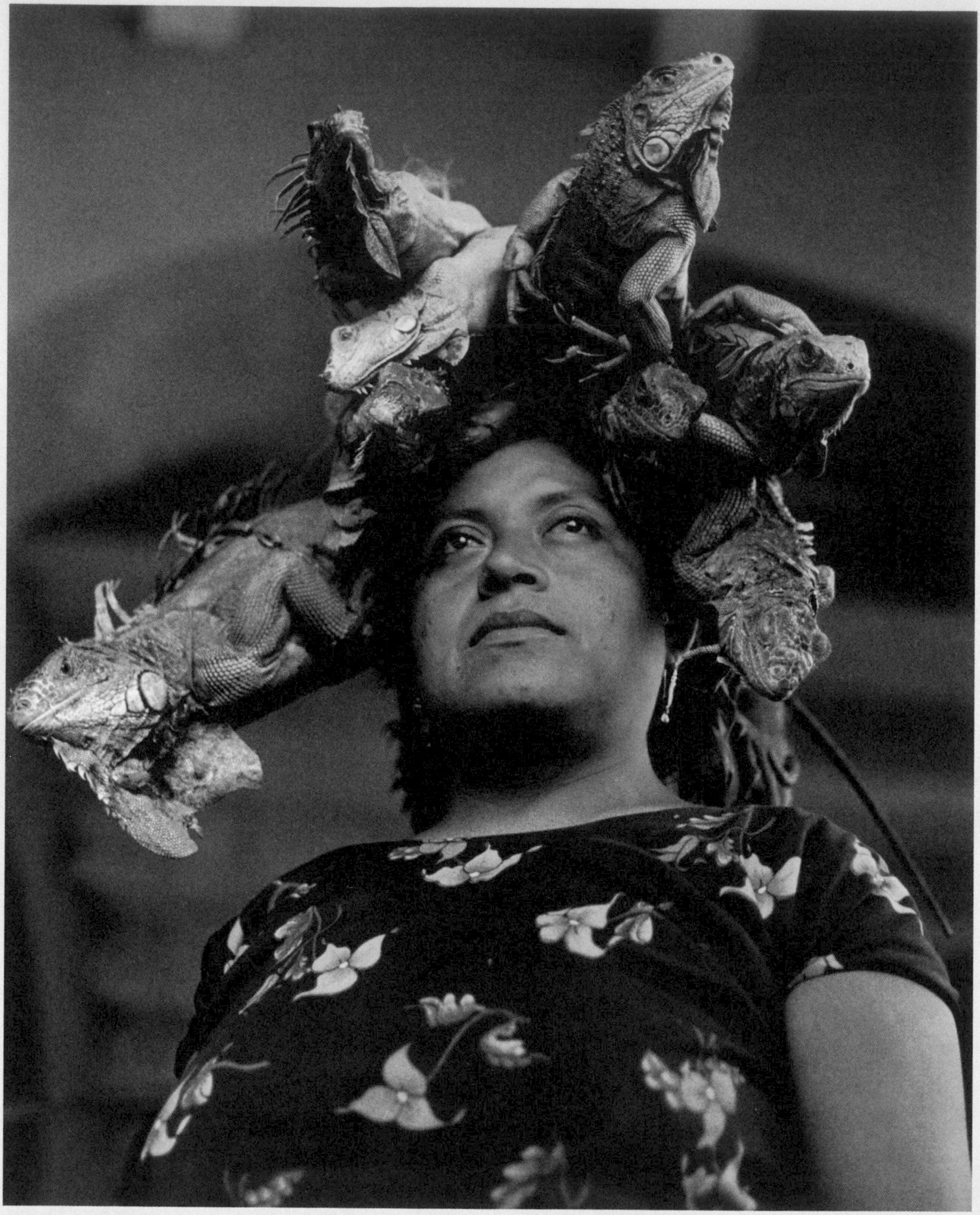

With one photograph, Zobeida, Juchitán, and I blur the line between the present and the mythical and immortal.

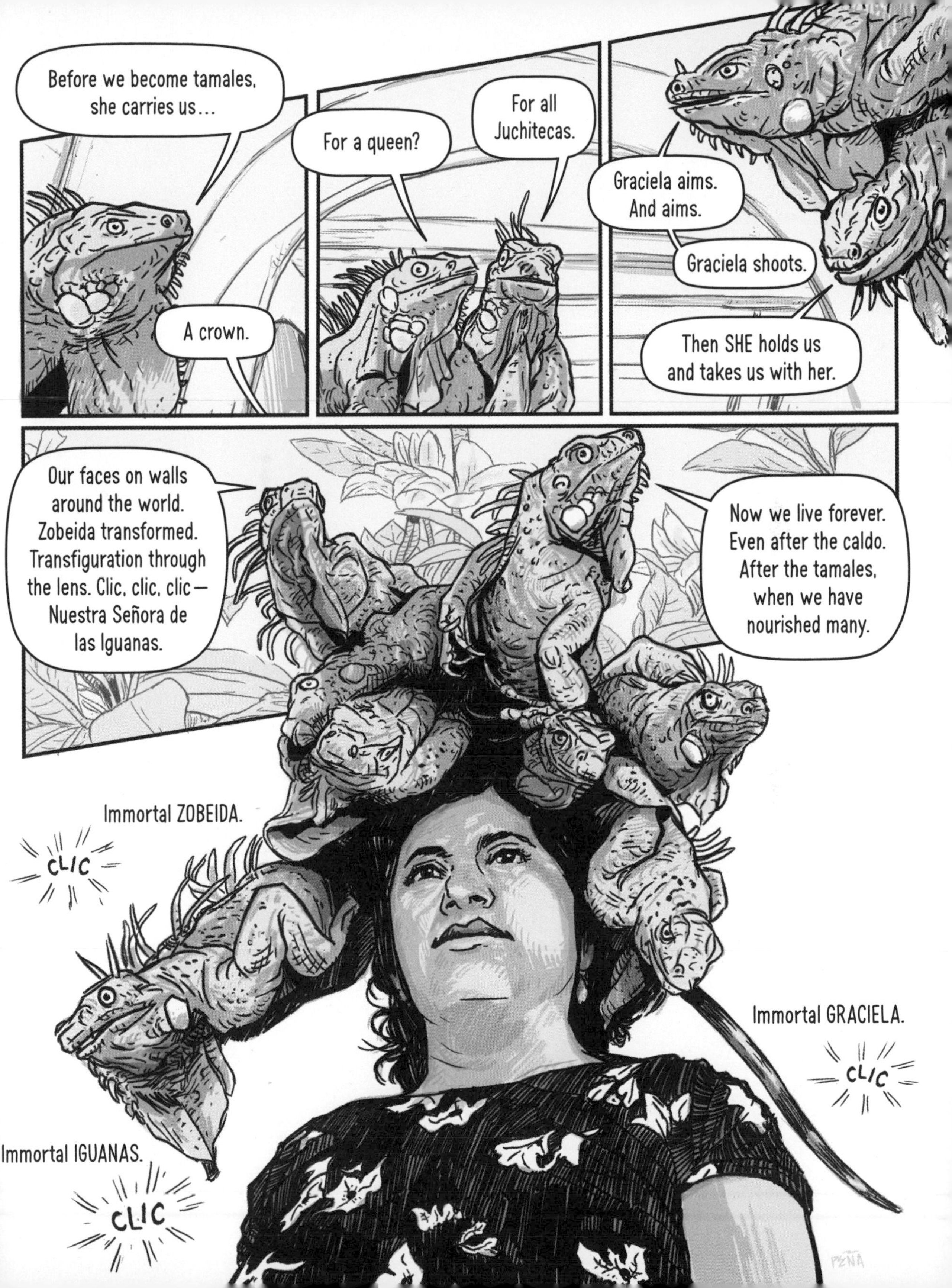

Before we become tamales, she carries us...
A crown.
For a queen?
For all Juchitecas.
Graciela aims. And aims.
Graciela shoots.
Then SHE holds us and takes us with her.
Our faces on walls around the world. Zobeida transformed. Transfiguration through the lens. Clic, clic, clic— Nuestra Señora de las Iguanas.
Now we live forever. Even after the caldo. After the tamales, when we have nourished many.
Immortal ZOBEIDA.
CLIC
Immortal GRACIELA.
CLIC
Immortal IGUANAS.
CLIC
PEÑA

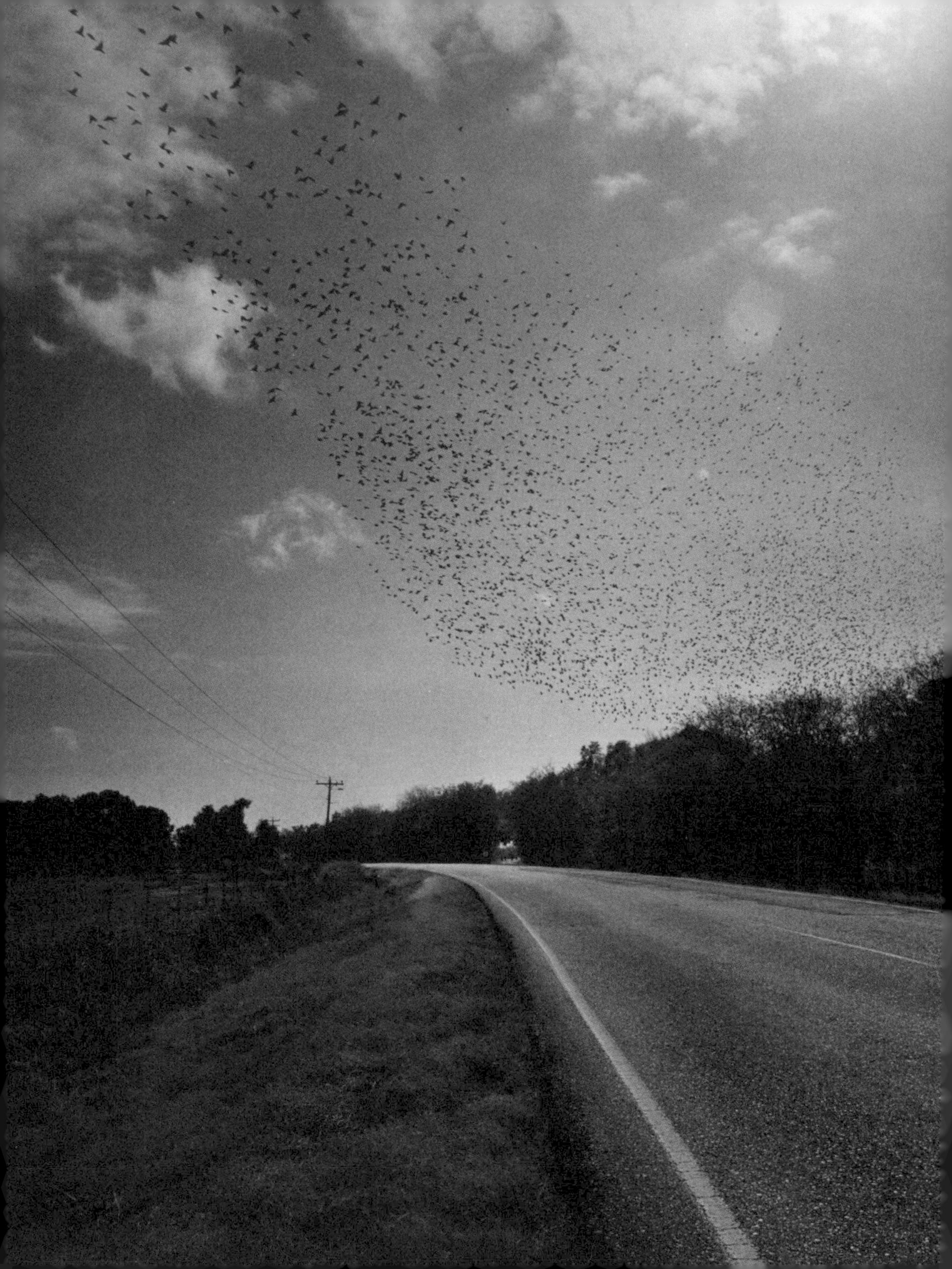

TRAVELING feeds the aviary that lives inside Graciela.

It keeps the restlessness at bay. Isn't that strange? To keep the birds still she must always be moving. Often she travels alone, though once in a while her sons go with her, and they take in the world together. Another set of eyes and good company.

When she goes to India for the first time, she takes her sons with her. Graciela was there for a book project. She and two other photographers (Sebastião Salgado and Raghu Rai) were asked to look for the links between Mexico and India. She realizes that the countries are not as similar as she once believed.

Do we force our vision to find likeness, Reader, because we fear difference? Or is there beauty in the difference—and in learning how we live and breathe and thrive amid all that difference?

Like when the University of Florida asked her to make a portrait of the United States. What would she find there that another photographer might not? What did the empty landscape of the South say to her? How did she learn to listen?

EL NORTE.

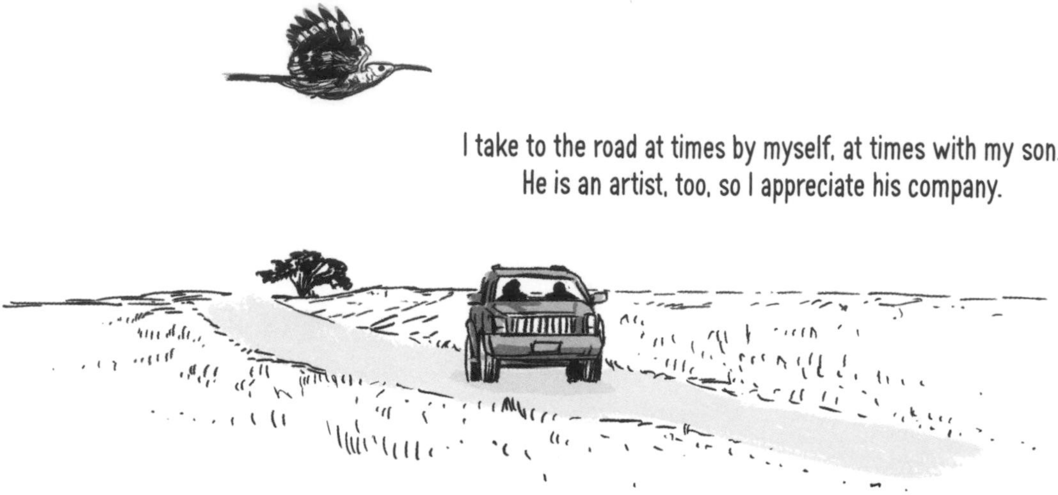
I take to the road at times by myself, at times with my son.
He is an artist, too, so I appreciate his company.

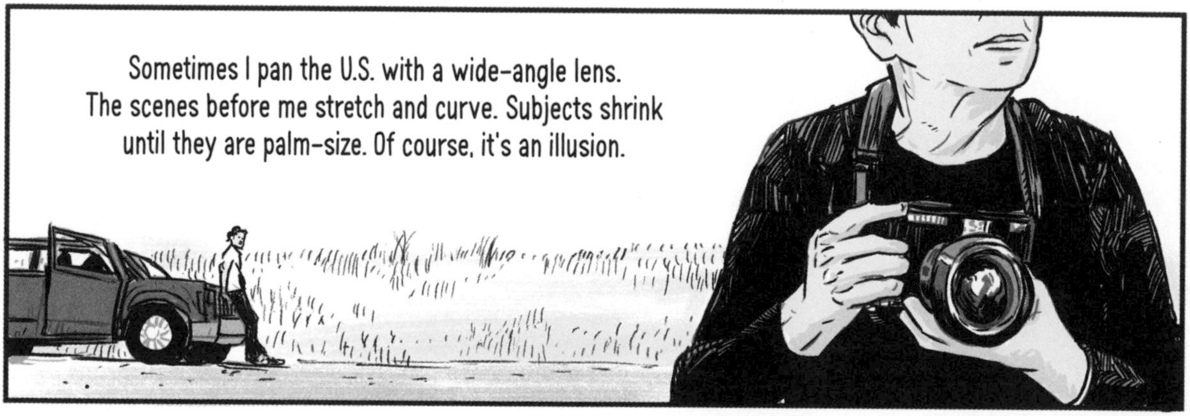
Sometimes I pan the U.S. with a wide-angle lens.
The scenes before me stretch and curve. Subjects shrink
until they are palm-size. Of course, it's an illusion.

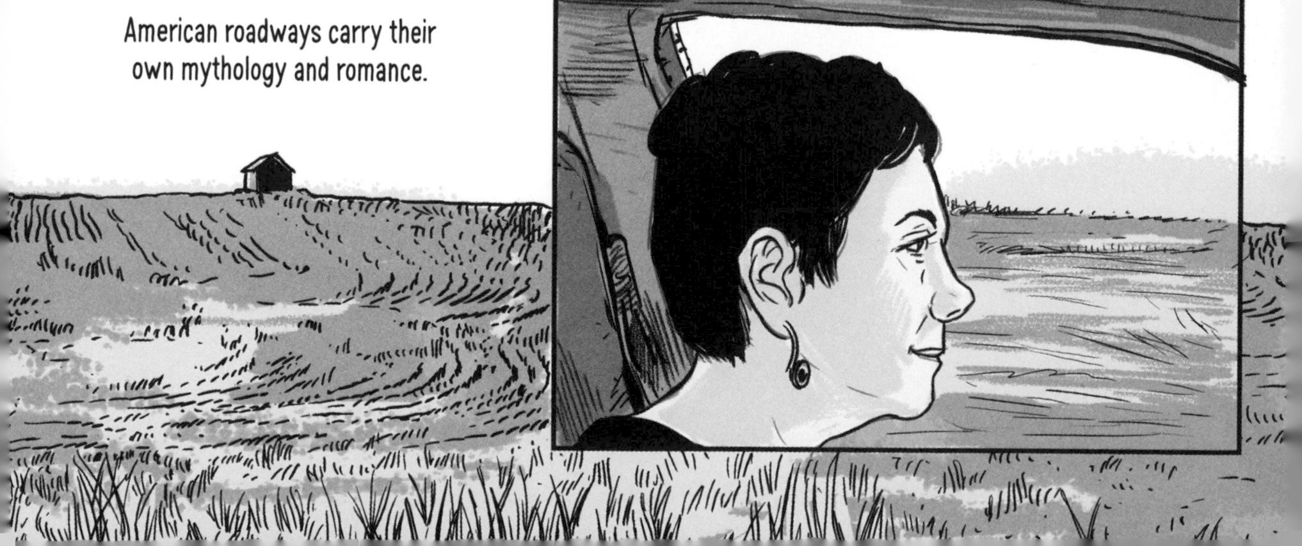
American roadways carry their
own mythology and romance.

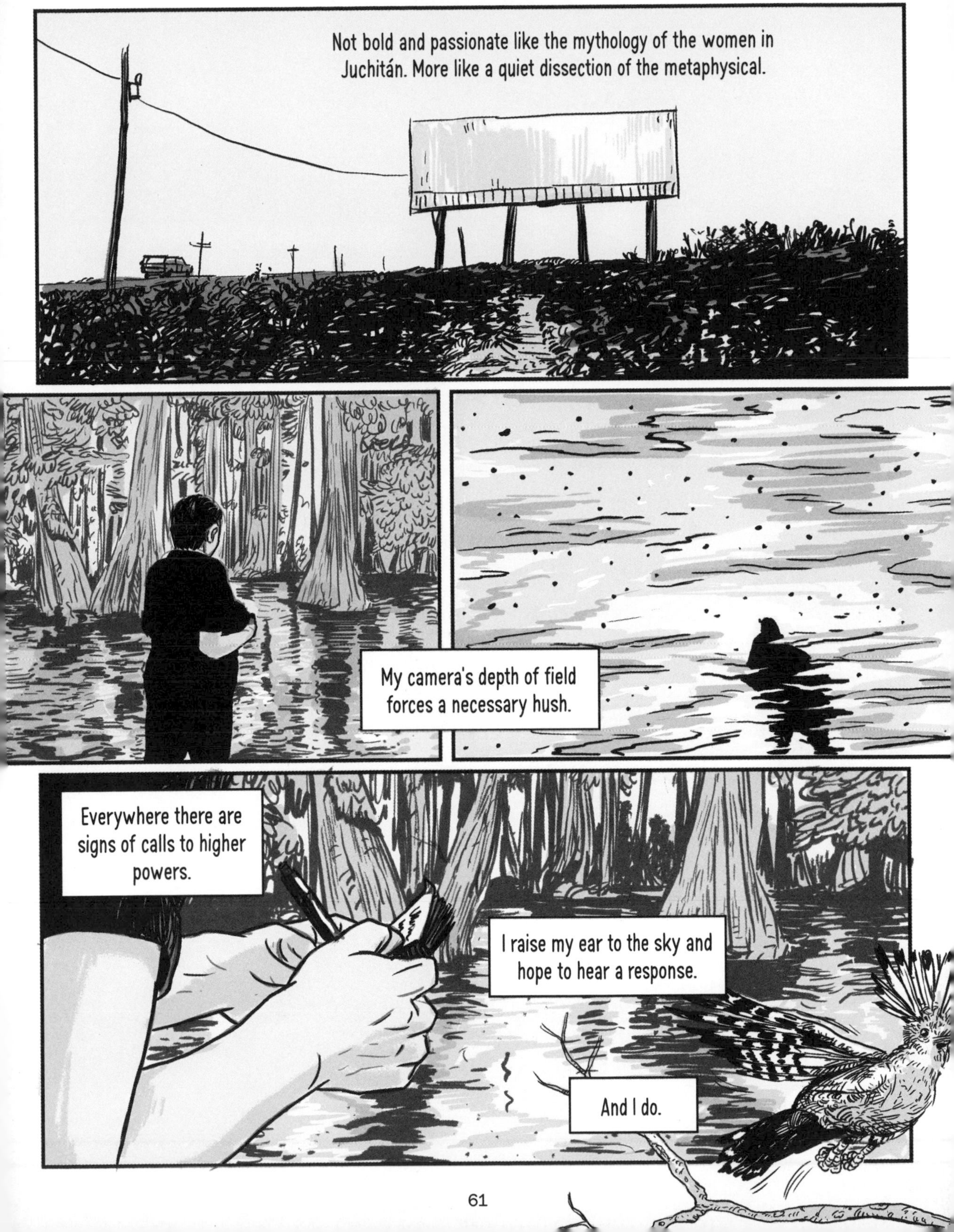
Not bold and passionate like the mythology of the women in Juchitán. More like a quiet dissection of the metaphysical.
My camera's depth of field forces a necessary hush.
Everywhere there are signs of calls to higher powers.
I raise my ear to the sky and hope to hear a response.
And I do.

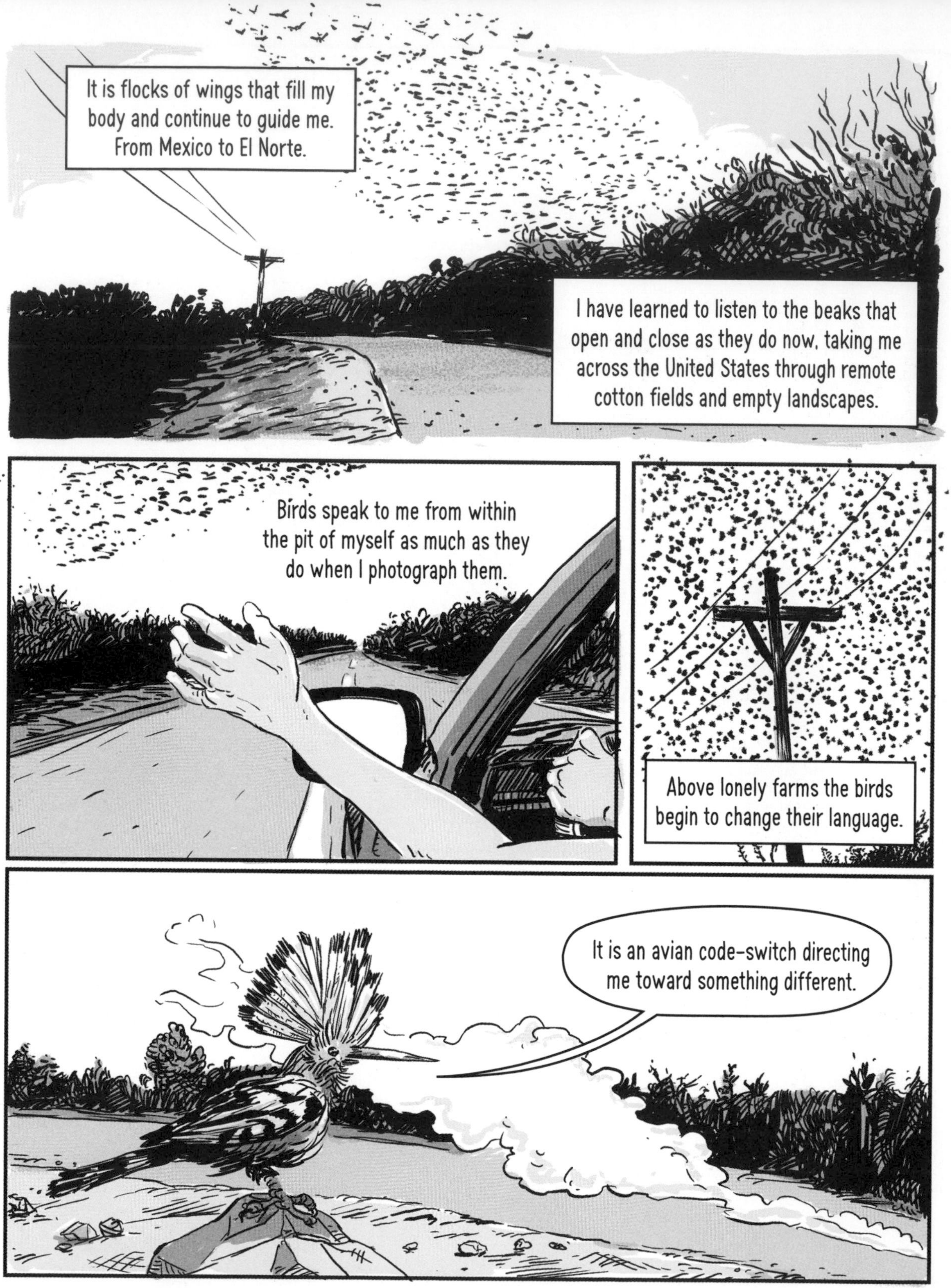
It is flocks of wings that fill my body and continue to guide me. From Mexico to El Norte.
I have learned to listen to the beaks that open and close as they do now, taking me across the United States through remote cotton fields and empty landscapes.
Birds speak to me from within the pit of myself as much as they do when I photograph them.
Above lonely farms the birds begin to change their language.
It is an avian code-switch directing me toward something different.

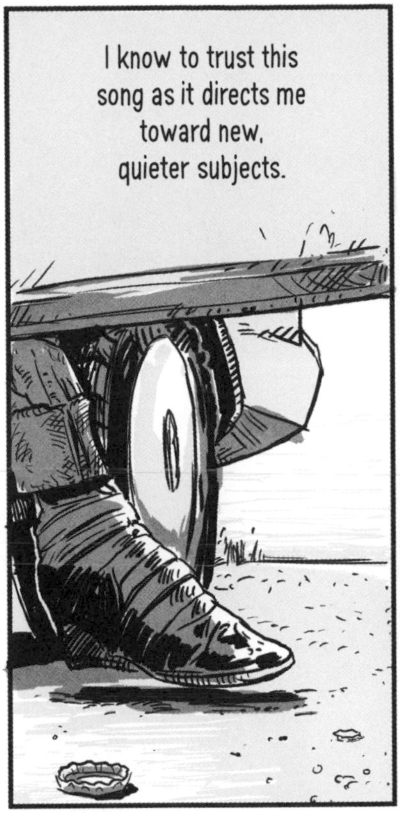
I know to trust this song as it directs me toward new, quieter subjects.

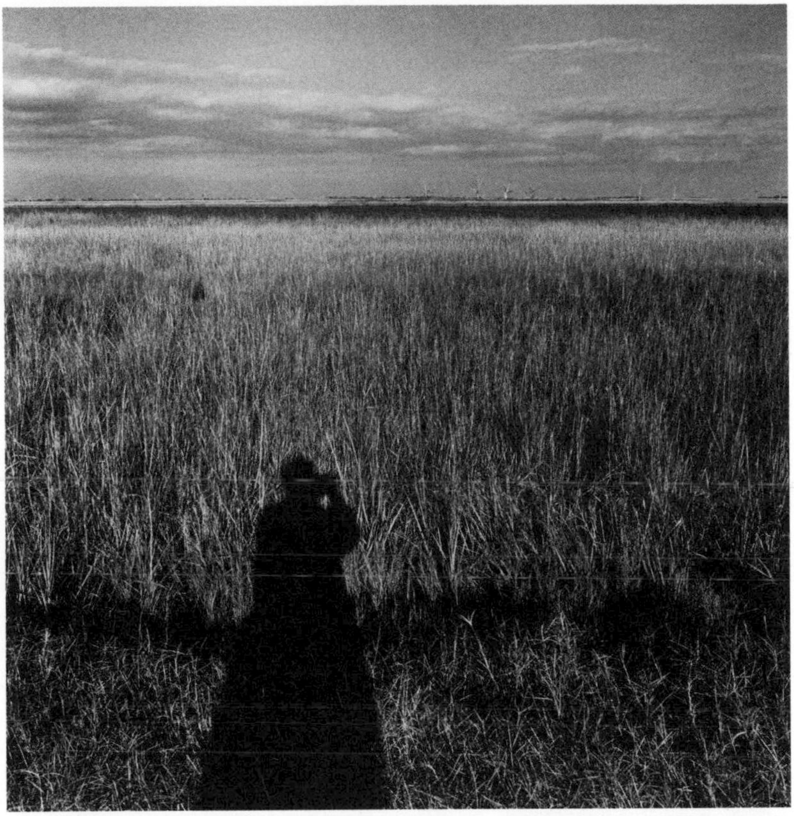

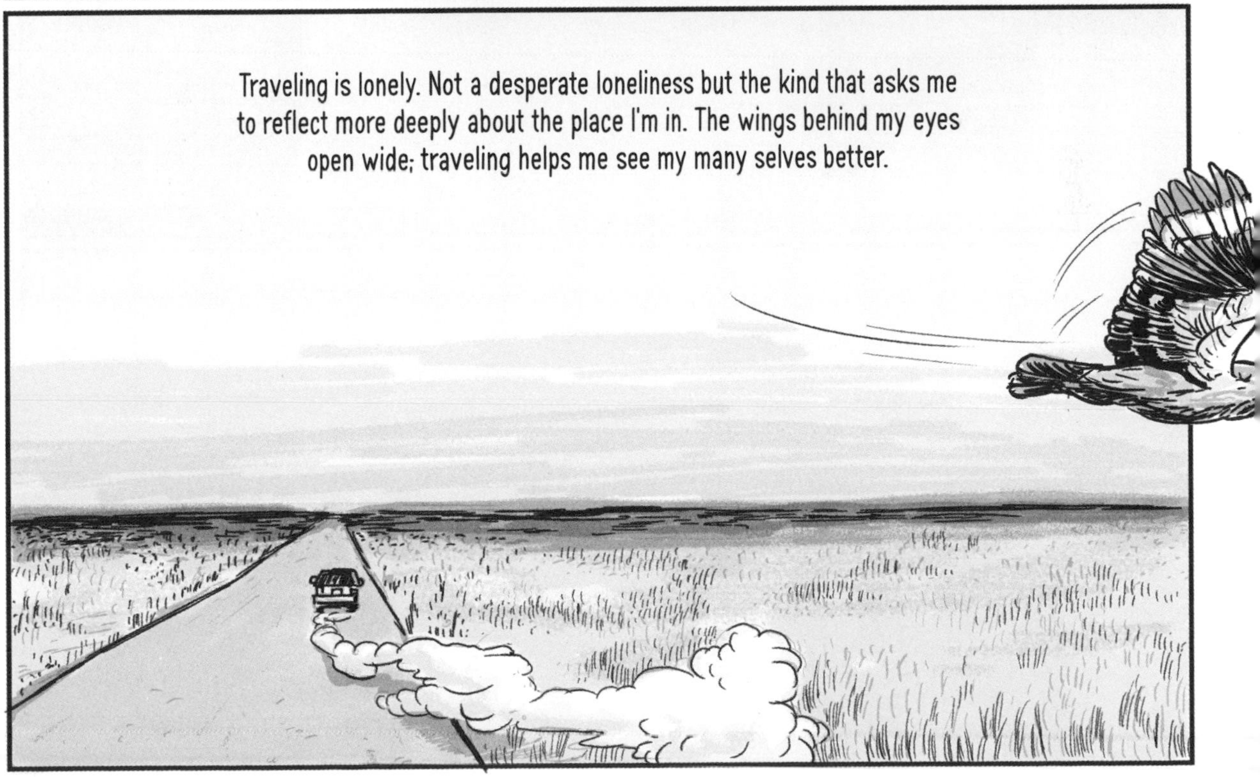
Traveling is lonely. Not a desperate loneliness but the kind that asks me to reflect more deeply about the place I'm in. The wings behind my eyes open wide; traveling helps me see my many selves better.

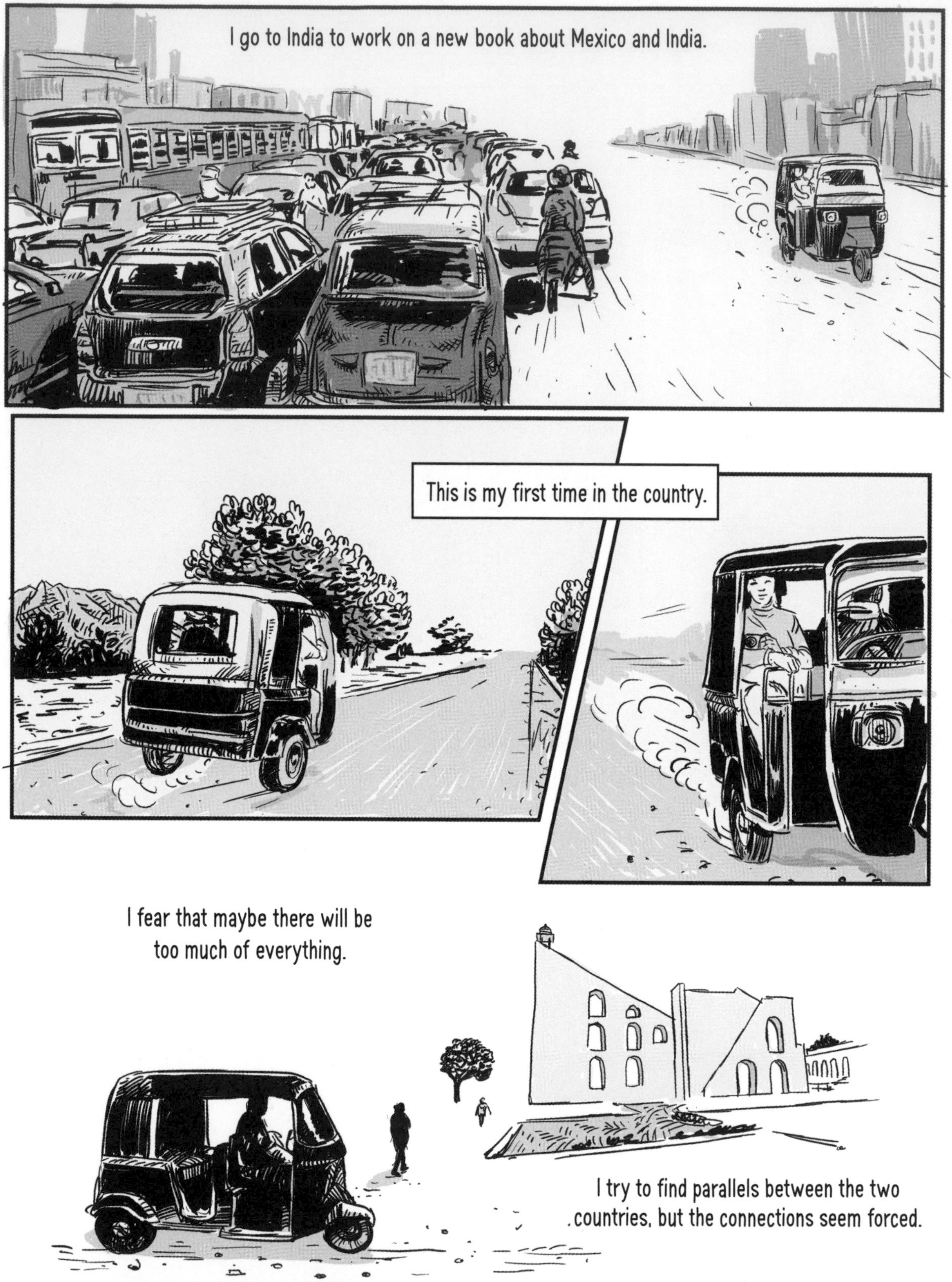

I go to India to work on a new book about Mexico and India.
This is my first time in the country.
I fear that maybe there will be too much of everything.
I try to find parallels between the two countries, but the connections seem forced.

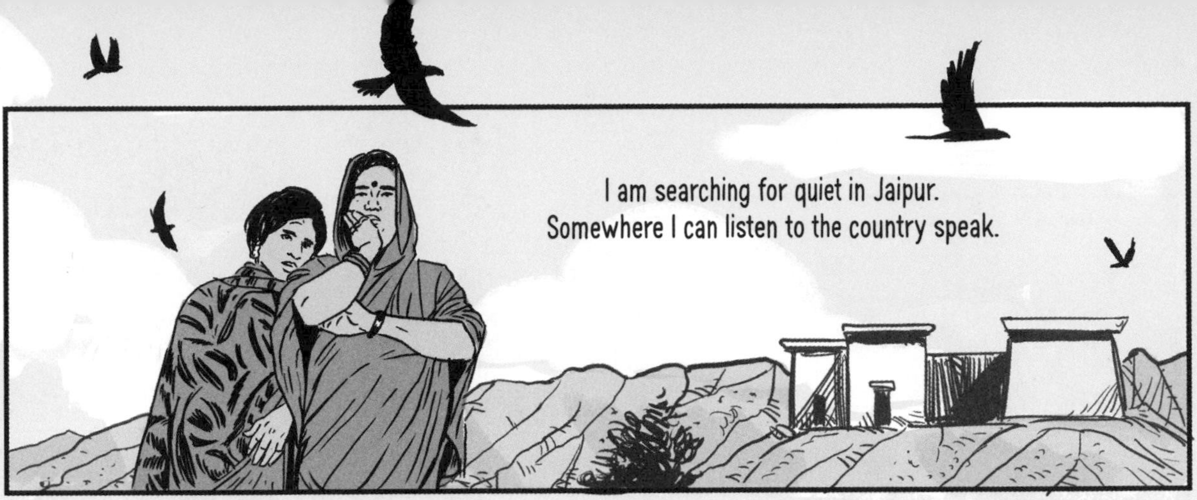
I am searching for quiet in Jaipur.
Somewhere I can listen to the country speak.

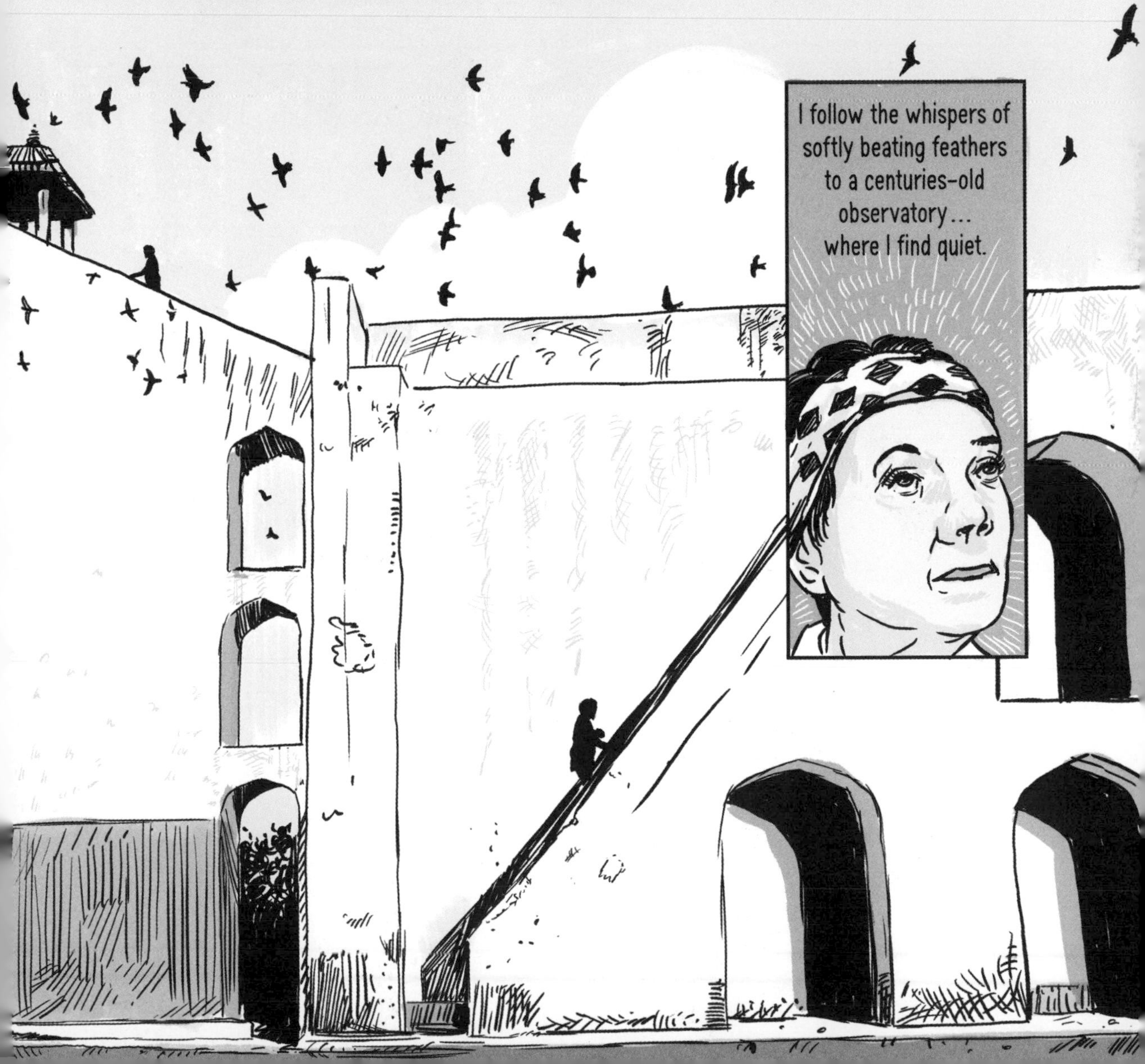
I follow the whispers of
softly beating feathers
to a centuries-old
observatory...
where I find quiet.

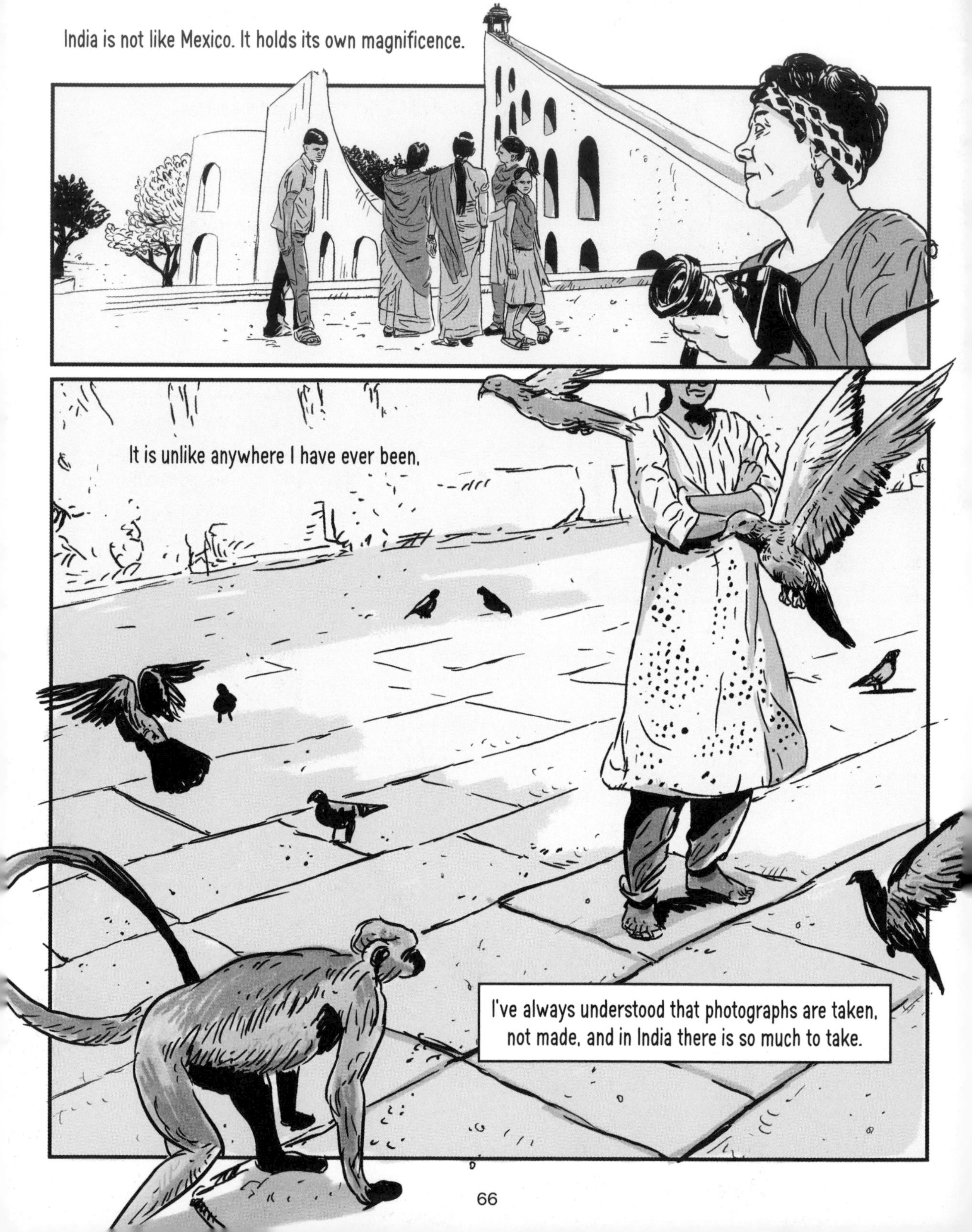
India is not like Mexico. It holds its own magnificence.
It is unlike anywhere I have ever been.
I've always understood that photographs are taken, not made, and in India there is so much to take.

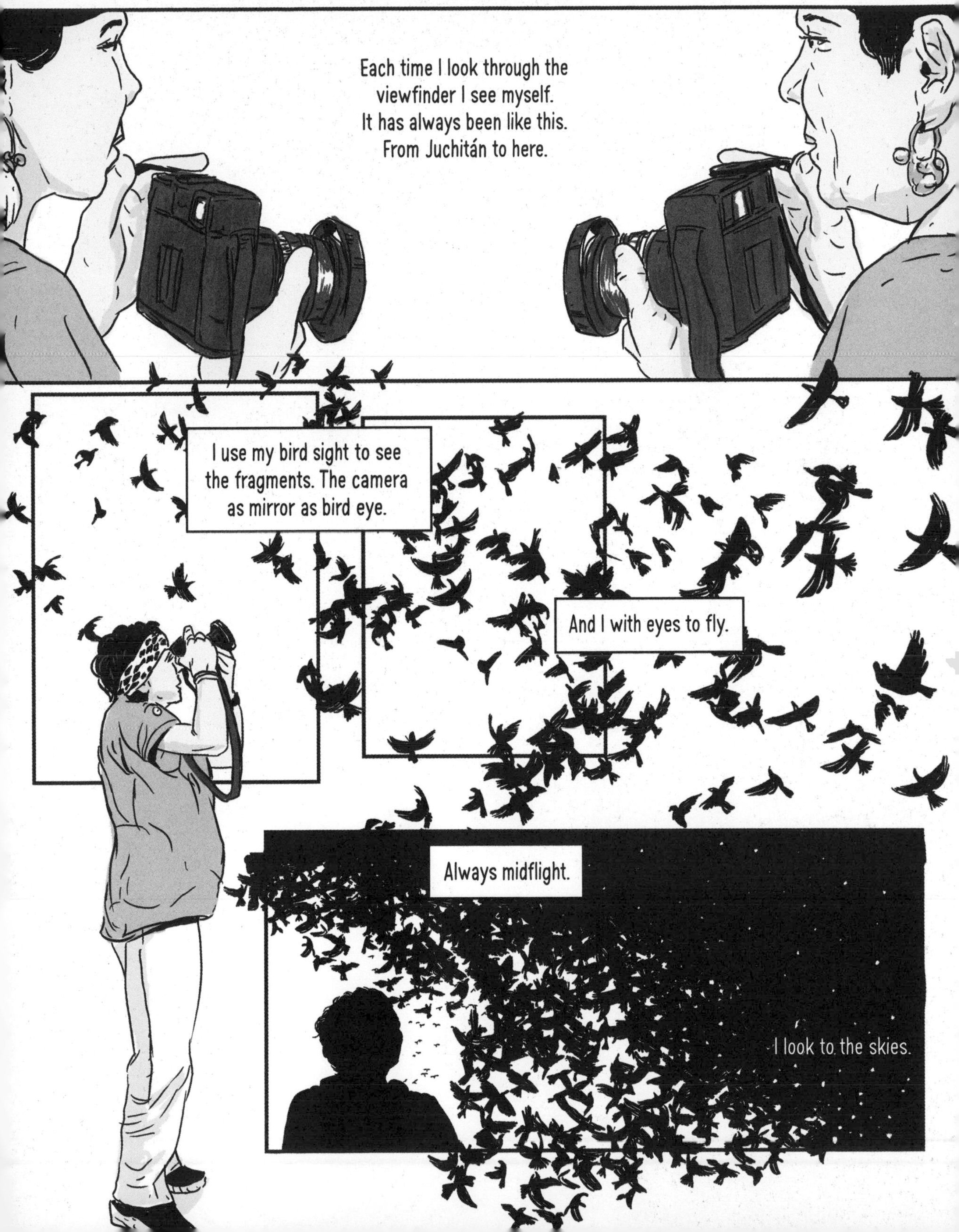

Each time I look through the viewfinder I see myself. It has always been like this. From Juchitán to here.
I use my bird sight to see the fragments. The camera as mirror as bird eye.
And I with eyes to fly.
Always midflight.
I look to the skies.

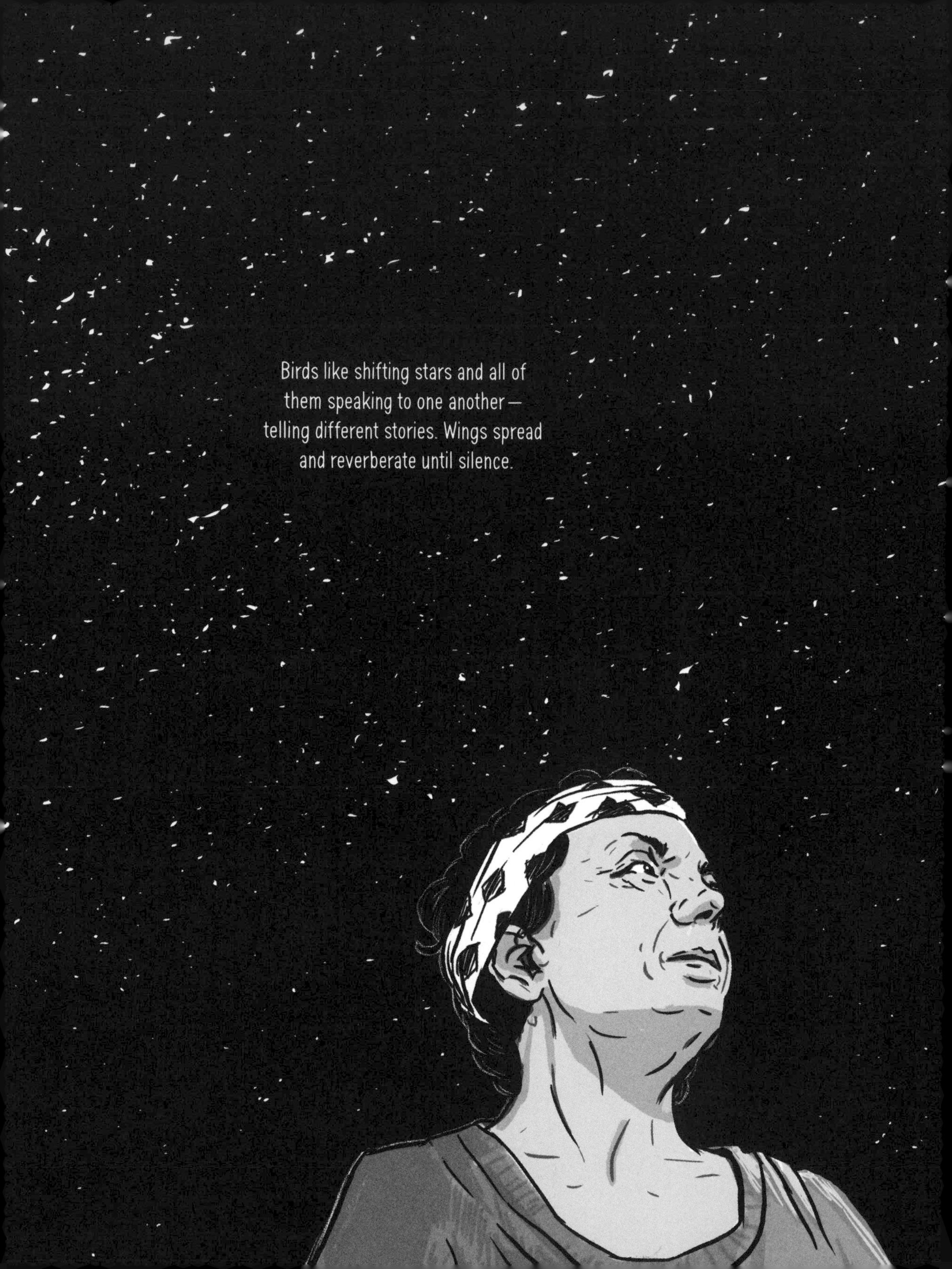
Birds like shifting stars and all of them speaking to one another—telling different stories. Wings spread and reverberate until silence.

Excuse me . . .

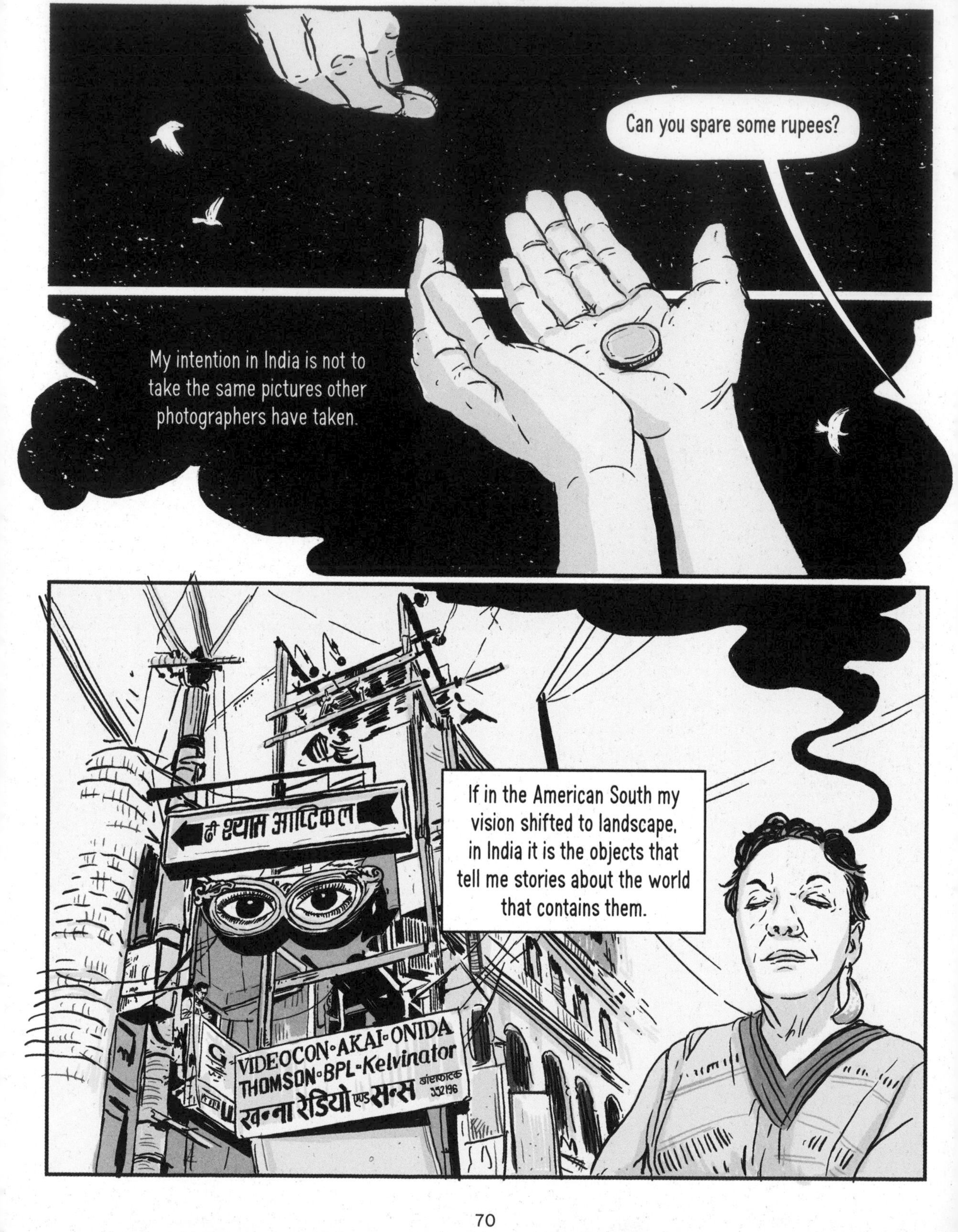
Can you spare some rupees?
My intention in India is not to take the same pictures other photographers have taken.
दी श्याम आप्टिकल
VIDEOCON•AKAI•ONIDA
THOMSON•BPL•Kelvinator
खन्ना रेडियो एण्ड सन्स
If in the American South my vision shifted to landscape, in India it is the objects that tell me stories about the world that contains them.

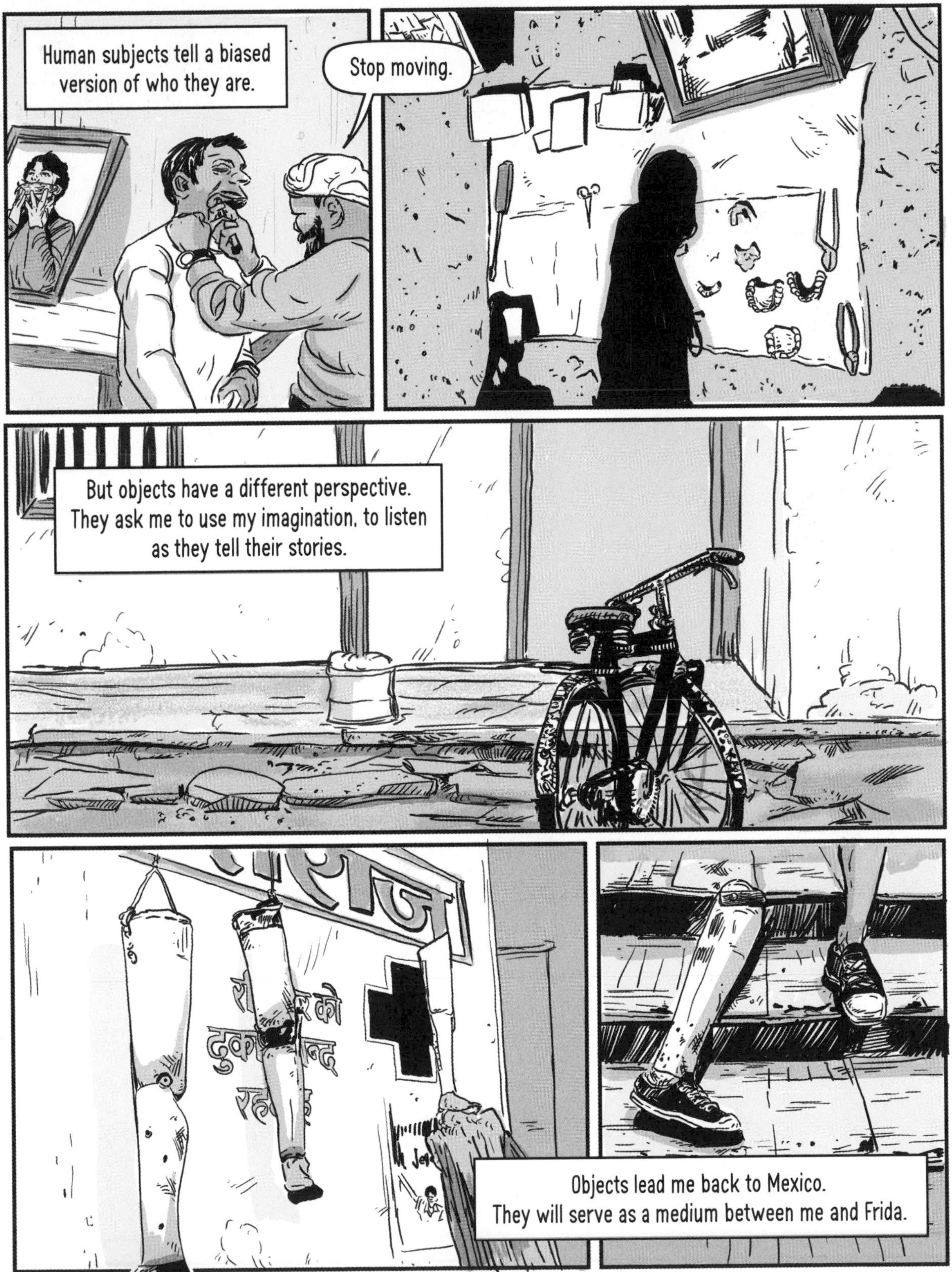
Human subjects tell a biased version of who they are.
Stop moving.
But objects have a different perspective. They ask me to use my imagination, to listen as they tell their stories.
Objects lead me back to Mexico.
They will serve as a medium between me and Frida.

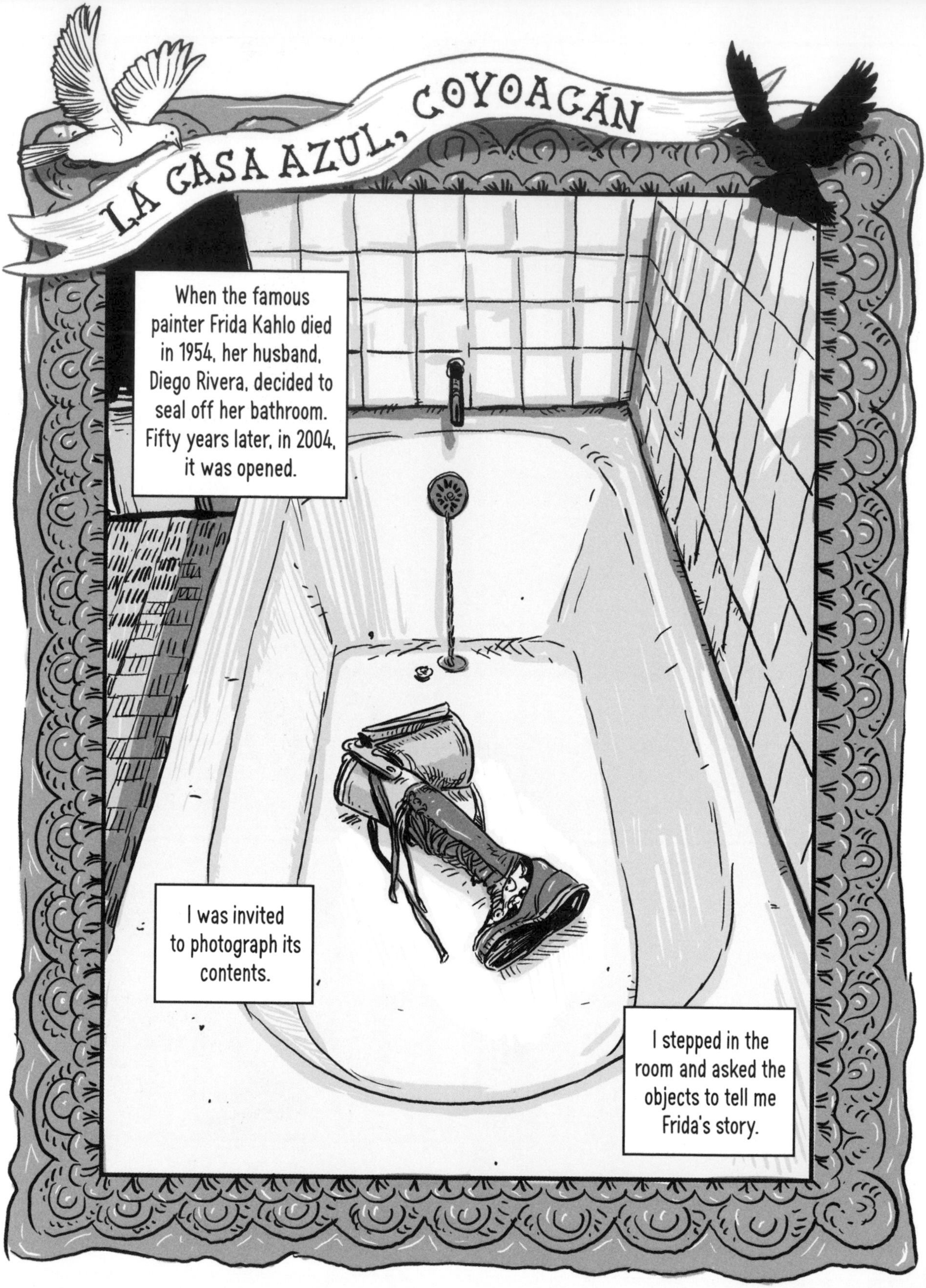
LA CASA AZUL, COYOACÁN
When the famous painter Frida Kahlo died in 1954, her husband, Diego Rivera, decided to seal off her bathroom. Fifty years later, in 2004, it was opened.
I was invited to photograph its contents.
I stepped in the room and asked the objects to tell me Frida's story.

I examine what Frida wanted to keep hidden—the braces and corsets and medications that allowed her to paint. It was an exhumation of a sacred space for private rituals.

I see a connection between my own question, "¿Ojos para volar?" and Frida's assertion that imagination is the ever-present pair of wings needed to claim freedom.

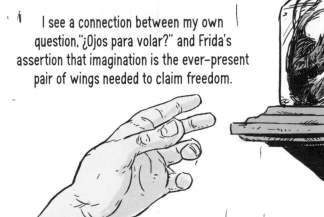

Birds. Always birds.

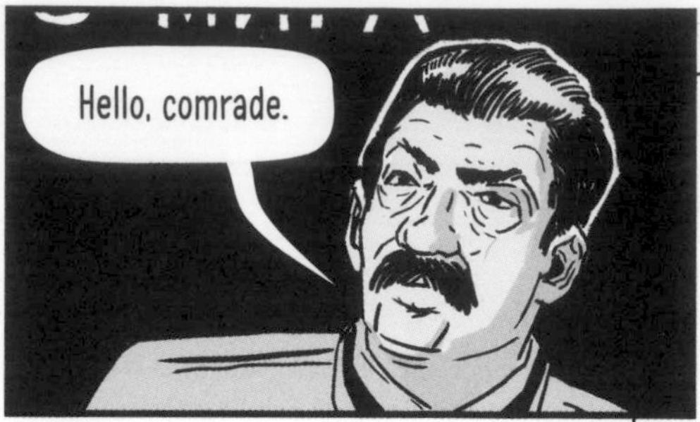
Hello, comrade.

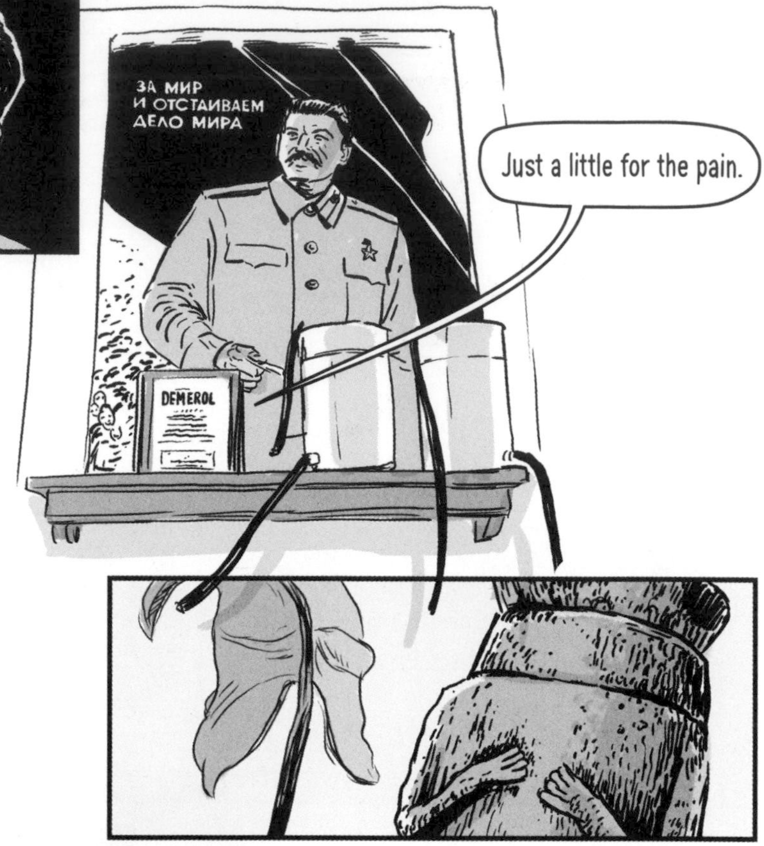
ЗА МИР
И ОТСТАИВАЕМ
ДЕЛО МИРА
Just a little for the pain.
DEMEROL

I arrange the objects in the bathroom to reimagine a story of a complicated artist. Stalin seems friendlier than he should, but what is he even doing here? The medicine I understand, but Stalin? What comfort could he have offered?

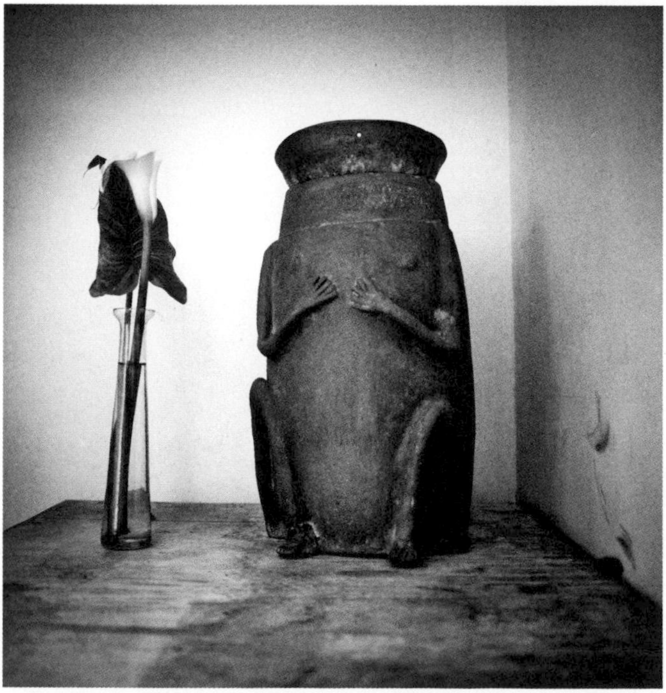

I get in trouble for moving Frida's ashes from her bedroom to her bathroom, reinterpreting their place in the house. It is a deliberate move of sacred remains contained in a pre-Hispanic object.

I gain a new admiration for Frida,
who created through pain.
Everywhere there's evidence of that pain
in the objects that held her together
until she unraveled.
But what beauty in the unraveling.

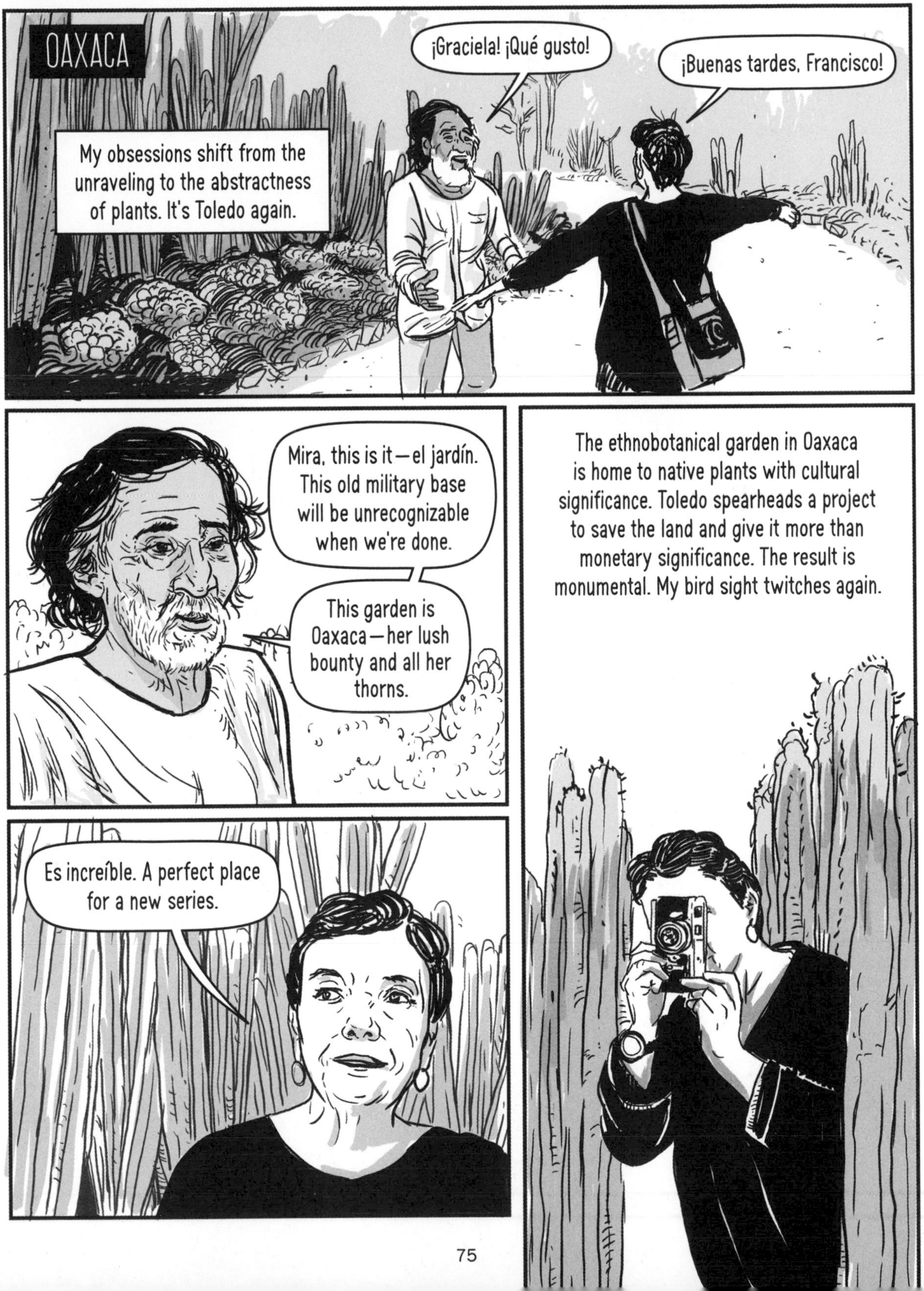
OAXACA
My obsessions shift from the unraveling to the abstractness of plants. It's Toledo again.
¡Graciela! ¡Qué gusto!
¡Buenas tardes, Francisco!
Mira, this is it—el jardín. This old military base will be unrecognizable when we're done.
This garden is Oaxaca—her lush bounty and all her thorns.
The ethnobotanical garden in Oaxaca is home to native plants with cultural significance. Toledo spearheads a project to save the land and give it more than monetary significance. The result is monumental. My bird sight twitches again.
Es increíble. A perfect place for a new series.

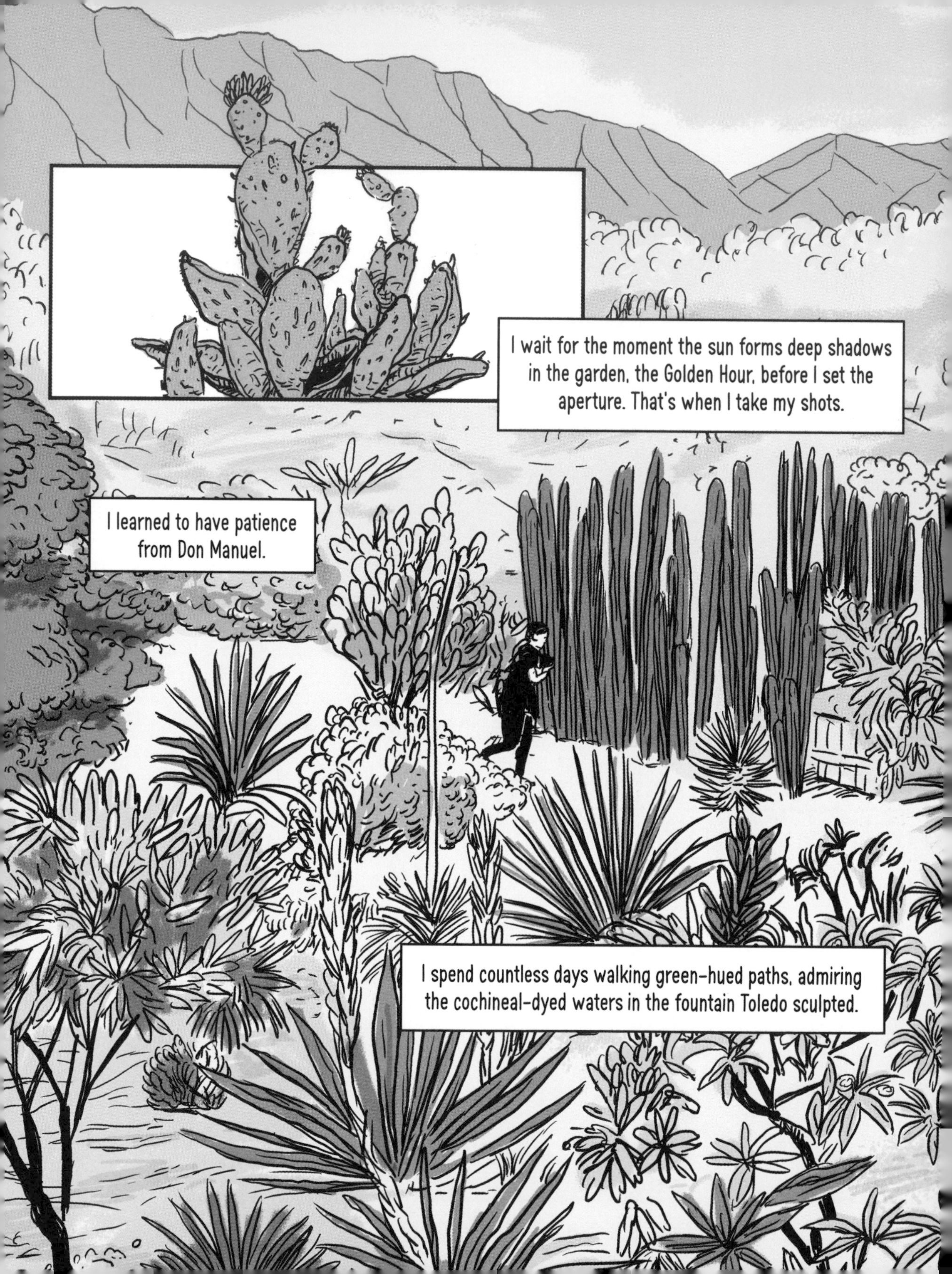
I wait for the moment the sun forms deep shadows in the garden, the Golden Hour, before I set the aperture. That's when I take my shots.
I learned to have patience from Don Manuel.
I spend countless days walking green-hued paths, admiring the cochineal-dyed waters in the fountain Toledo sculpted.

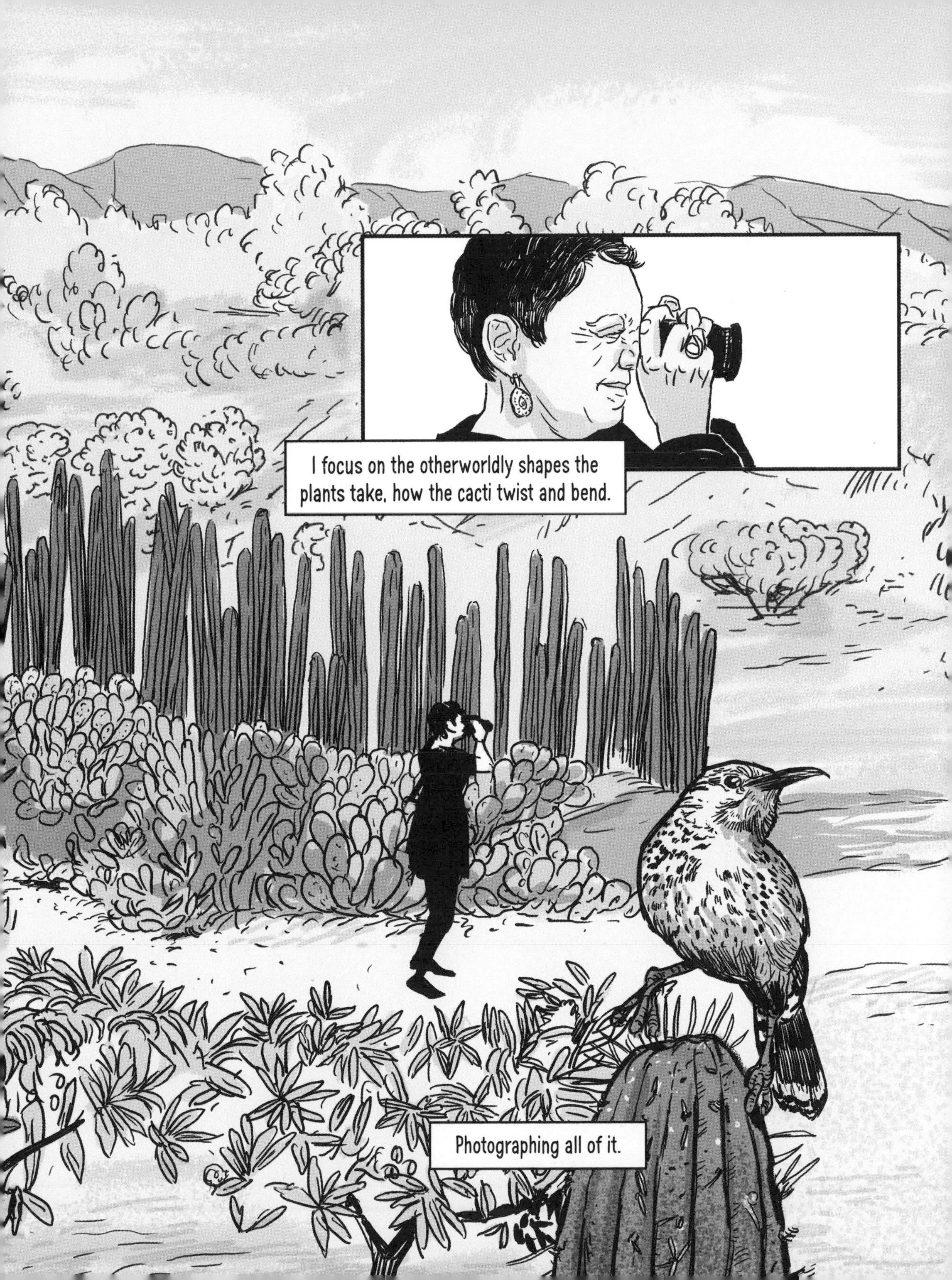
I focus on the otherworldly shapes the plants take, how the cacti twist and bend.
Photographing all of it.

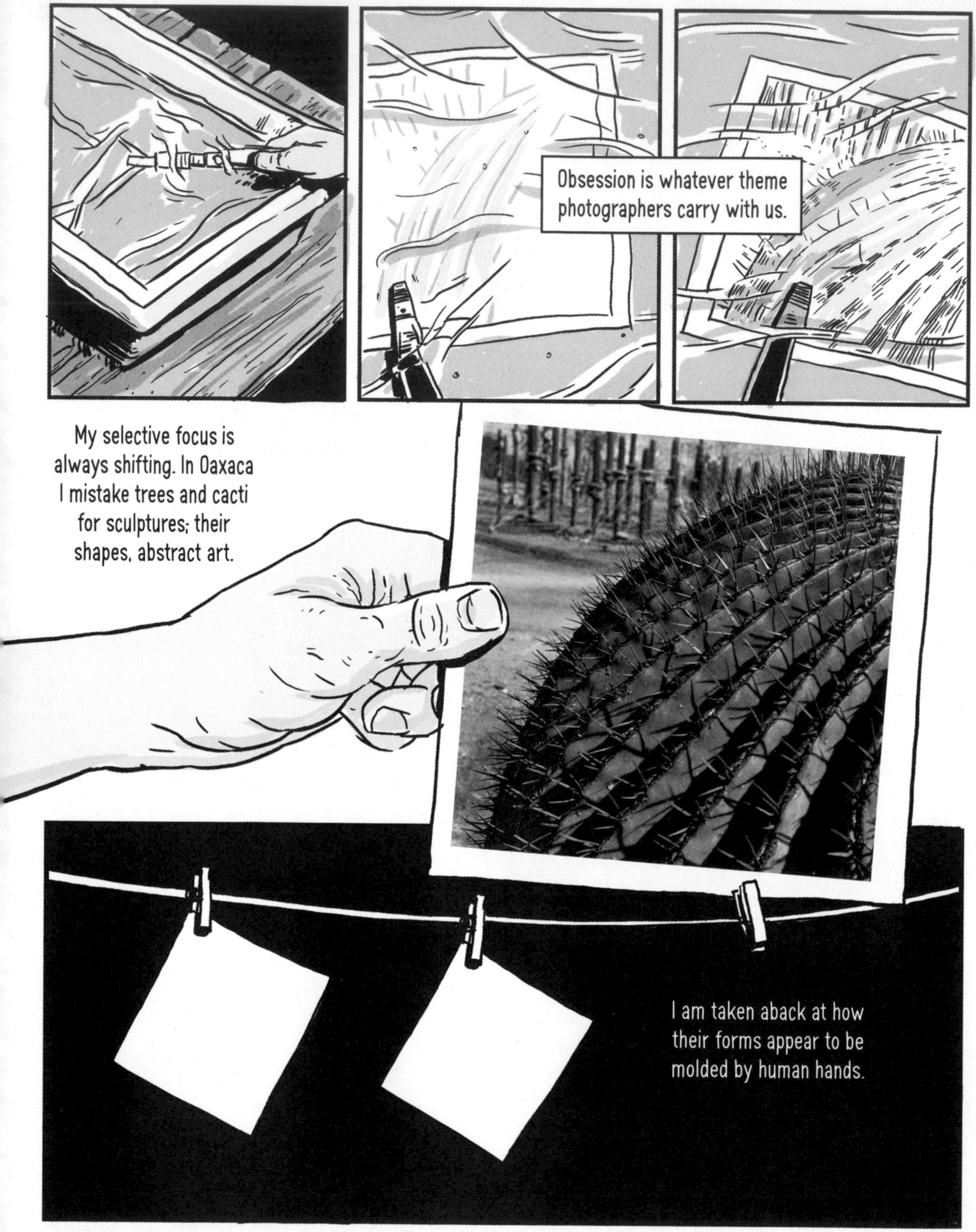
Obsession is whatever theme photographers carry with us.
My selective focus is always shifting. In Oaxaca I mistake trees and cacti for sculptures; their shapes, abstract art.
I am taken aback at how their forms appear to be molded by human hands.

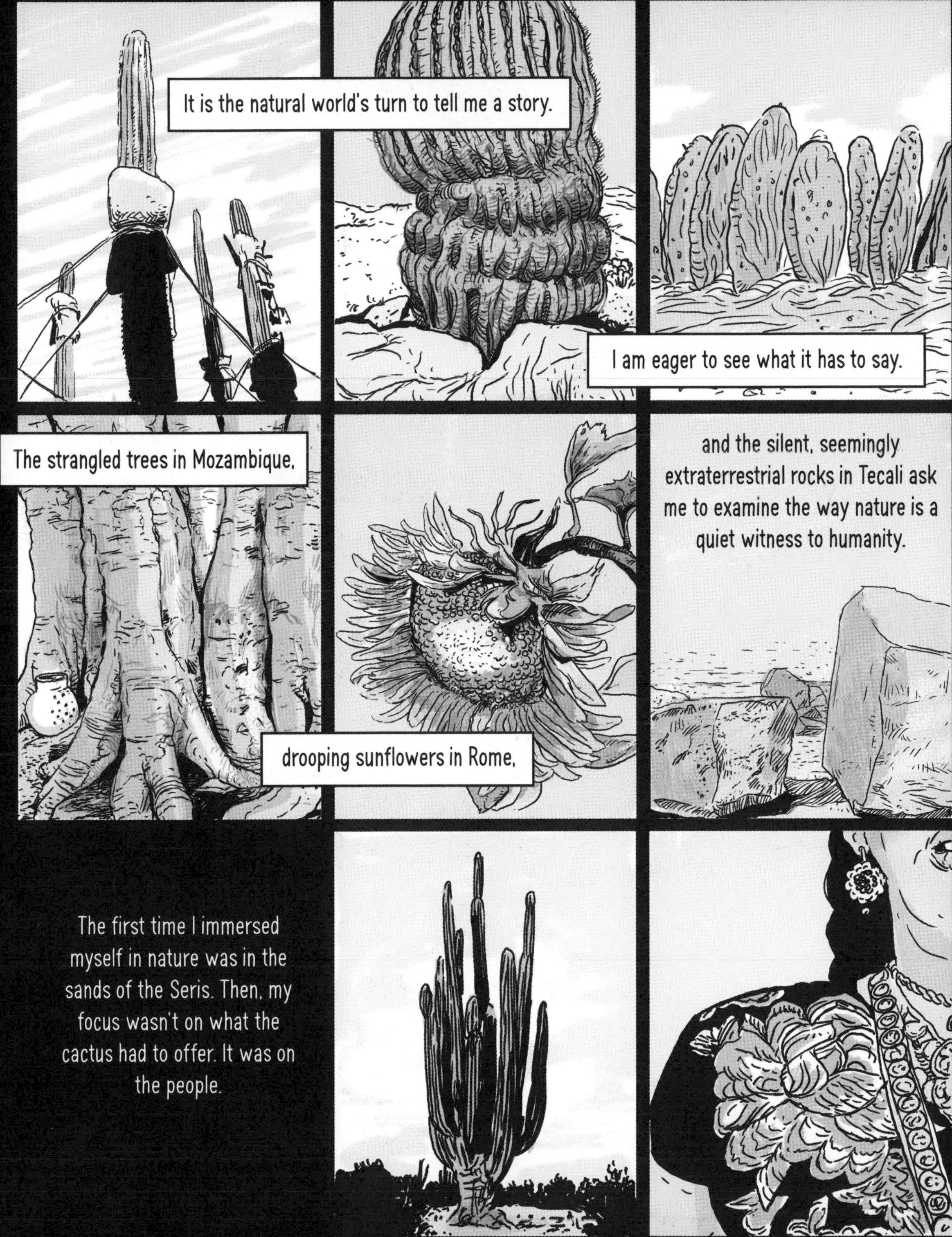
It is the natural world's turn to tell me a story.
I am eager to see what it has to say.
The strangled trees in Mozambique,
drooping sunflowers in Rome,
and the silent, seemingly extraterrestrial rocks in Tecali ask me to examine the way nature is a quiet witness to humanity.
The first time I immersed myself in nature was in the sands of the Seris. Then, my focus wasn't on what the cactus had to offer. It was on the people.

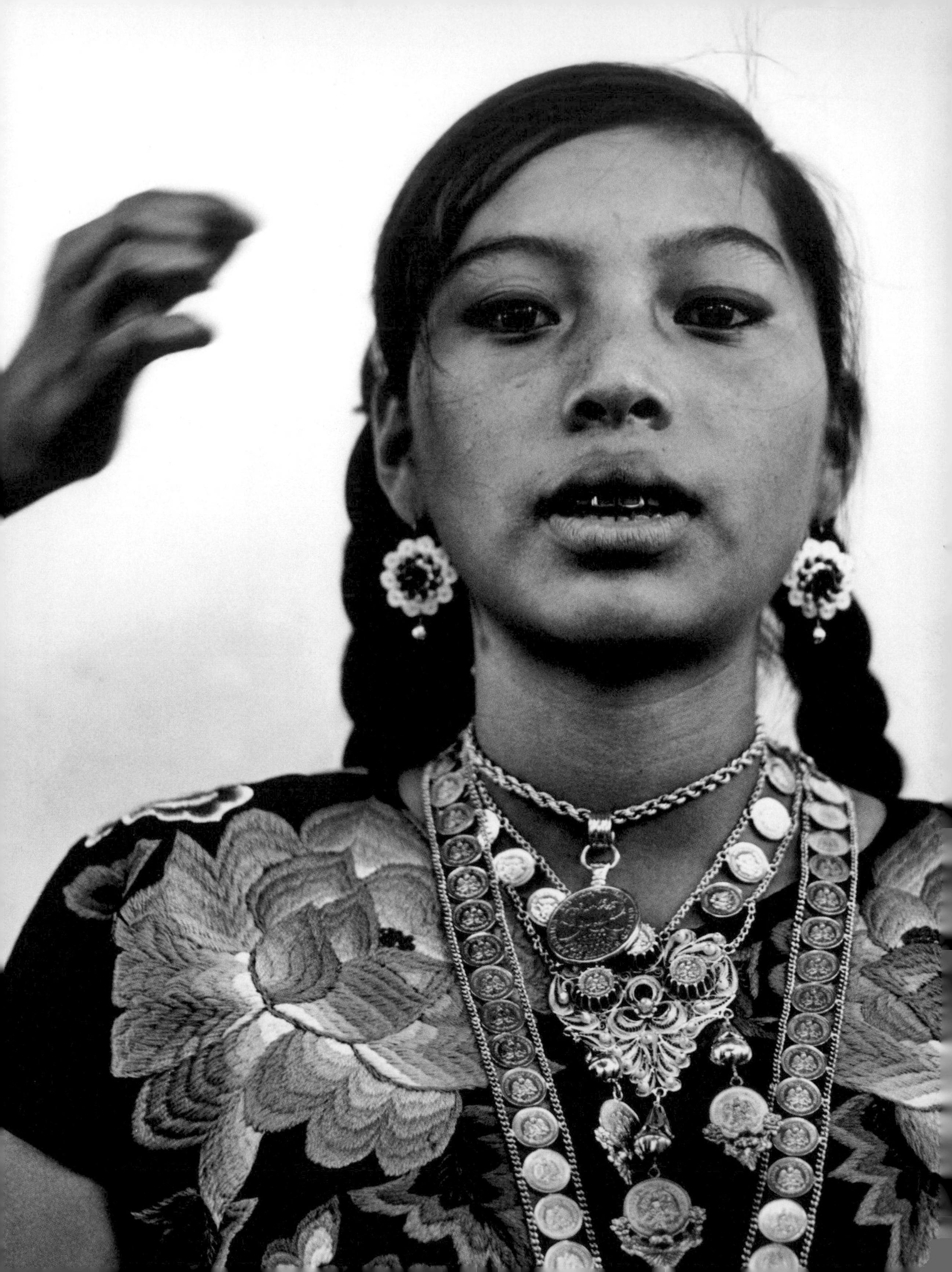

CHANGING OBSESSIONS make for good poems, and Graciela's work has been one long poem; each shift a line break, a new stanza, a turn. Each photograph a mirror, a reflection of how far the black sheep has come, and the sacrifice endured, to create a path for herself.

And yes, Reader, it feels like the end because it is the end. Of this book, that is—for Graciela still photographs. She never leaves her home without a camera. Her wings are spread and her eyes are always ready to fly. She does the same thing she's been doing for over forty years. Beginning in a desert many years ago. Most likely before you were born.

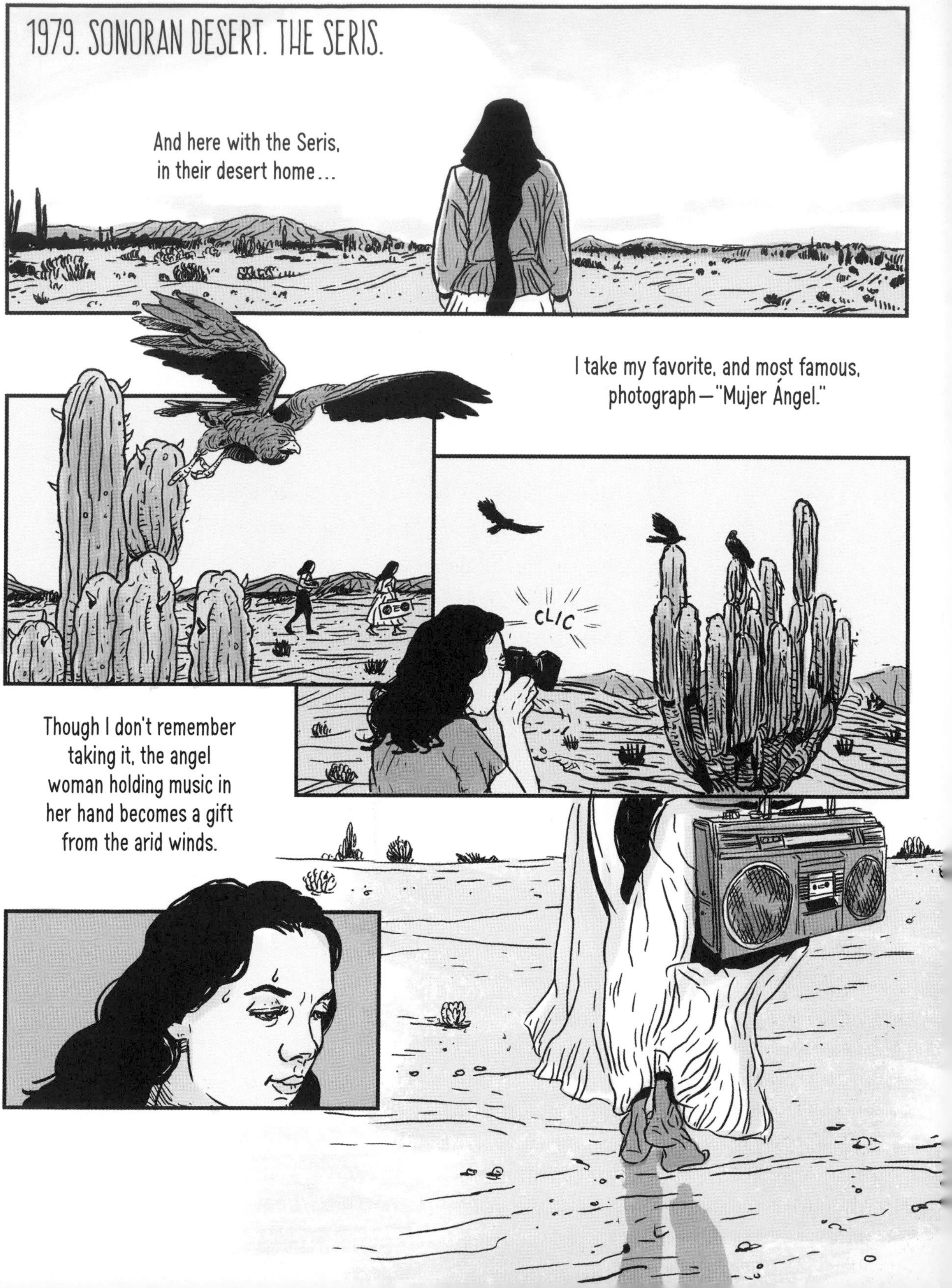
1979. SONORAN DESERT. THE SERIS.
And here with the Seris, in their desert home…
I take my favorite, and most famous, photograph—"Mujer Ángel."
CLIC
Though I don't remember taking it, the angel woman holding music in her hand becomes a gift from the arid winds.

It's proof of the present and past colliding.

It's like this: when I look at a subject, the subject must always look back. Must always agree with the shot.

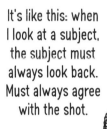

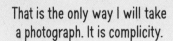

That is the only way I will take a photograph. It is complicity.

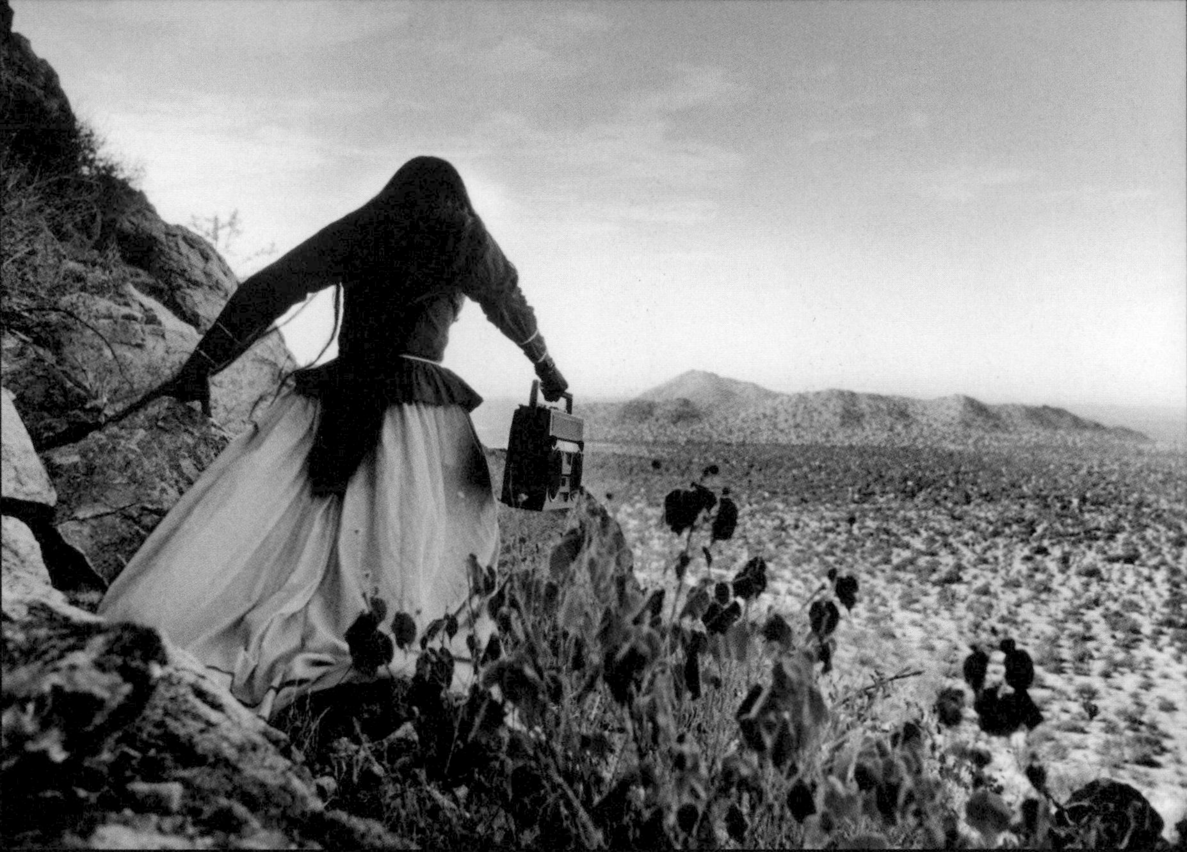

We are all fragments of one another,
strewn across Mexico and across borders.

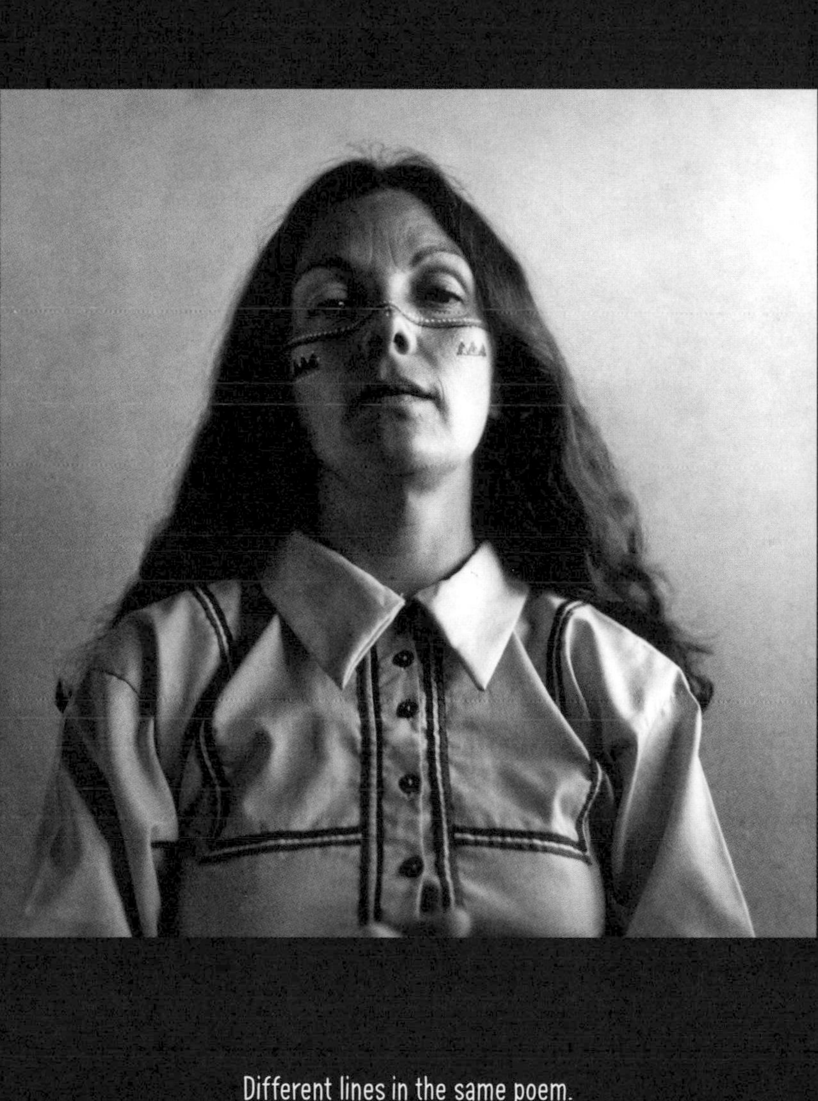

Different lines in the same poem.

Graciela still travels and exhibits her work all over the world.

She never leaves her home in Mexico City without a camera.

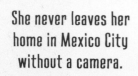

CLIC

From the moment her eyes grew wings, she has never stopped flying.

What the eye sees is the synthesis
of what you are or what you've learned to do.
This is the language of photography.

This is the language Graciela has become fluent in.

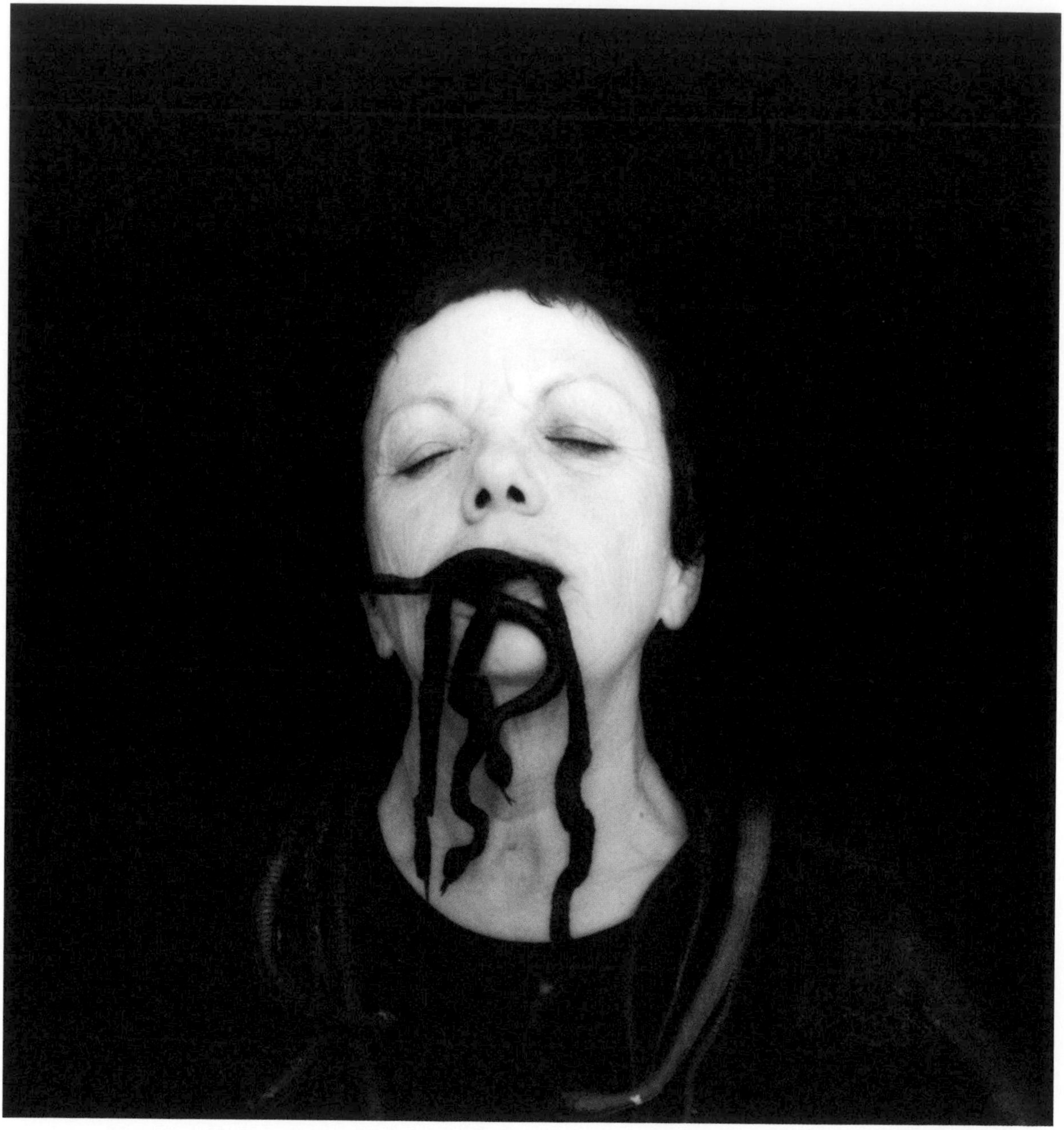

GRACIELA ITURBIDE BIOGRAPHY

Graciela Iturbide was born May 16, 1942, a few days before Mexico, her country of birth, entered World War II. She grew up in an upper-class home in Mexico City, the eldest of thirteen children. Her conservative Catholic family expected that Iturbide would marry and have children, which she did. She married in 1962 and had a daughter and two sons. Then in 1969 she enrolled at the Universidad Nacional Autónoma de México to study film—a courageous decision for a young woman from a traditional family. After the death of her daughter in 1970, she took a course with famed Mexican photographer Manuel Álvarez Bravo and became interested in still photography. Ultimately, her marriage ended, and Iturbide embraced her new life as an artist.

Álvarez Bravo took on Iturbide as pupil and assistant—his achichincle. From him she learned not only how to photograph but also how to live and to maintain a lifelong appetite for learning, especially literature. Álvarez Bravo was part of the radical artistic communities of the 1920s, including Tina Modotti, Diego Rivera, and Frida Kahlo, whose works celebrated Mexico's rich indigenous cultures. Like that of his contemporaries, Álvarez Bravo's work often captures indigenous people and campesinos—subjects he encouraged Iturbide to explore. Though one can see traces of his influence in her photographs, Iturbide began to move away from her mentor's legacy. Iturbide has a different way of looking at Mexico; she is concerned with not only *documenting* Mexican life but also providing a background made up of its various histories. This mixture of the indigenous and postcolonial she calls "Mexican Tempo."

Iturbide's other great influence is her contemporary, the Zapotec artist Francisco Toledo. A painter, printmaker, and sculptor, Toledo was born in Juchitán de Zaragoza, a place he would later invite Iturbide to photograph. In addition to being a mentor, Toledo has been a lifelong friend. Many years after she was divorced, Toledo painted a frog on Iturbide's head in her wedding photo, a symbol of her supposed prince turning into the proverbial frog. A gift from artist to artist, the painting sits in her bathroom, alongside much of her prized art collection. Toledo's work often revolves around mythologies and depicts animals. Though a world-renowned artist, Toledo keeps a close connection with his home state of Oaxaca through his activism and dedication to bringing arts to communities in the state, providing resources for burgeoning young artists.

Iturbide has been influenced by many practitioners: Tina Modotti, Henri Cartier-Bresson, and Brassaï. These photographers have helped her define her artistic vision. Brassaï once wrote that "life cannot be captured by realism or naturalism, but only through dreams, symbols, or the imagination," an idea that resonates deeply for Iturbide. The photograph *Señor de los Pájaros* was taken after a recurring dream of a man surrounded by birds. She then encountered that very man in Las Islas Marías, capturing her dreams on film. Neither the dream nor photograph could exist without each other. *Nuestra Señora de las Iguanas* (on page 56) is reminiscent of Medusa, the Gorgon of Greek mythology, and yet it captures the day-to-day reality of a woman bringing iguanas to sell at the market. This is not to say that Iturbide stages photographs, because that would be inaccurate—she never does. Instead, it is as if Brassaï's words and art subconsciously inform the way she captures images, as she encounters her subjects and presses down on the shutter release.

It's tempting to call Iturbide's photographs "surreal" or "magical"—both terms she rejects. In an interview, Iturbide said, "I don't like it when they refer to my work as being magical—it makes me furious. It would interest me more, and I don't know if I ever will get there, if my work had some poetic qualities." Her work contains rhythm, metaphor, and an insistence on better understanding herself and the world she exists in. Her photography answers Brassaï's call to capture life with dreams, symbolism, and imagination—with a camera. In her photographs of the slaughter of the goats (see pages 40–45), the Mixtecas' hands become a metaphor for Mexico, the goats' bleating a lyric. Iturbide's photography grounds itself in reality while simultaneously existing in that in-between space—the Mexican Tempo.

Throughout her career Iturbide has traveled the world, though some of her most famous works come from indigenous communities in Mexico: the Seris in Sonora and the Juchitecas in Oaxaca. She has won many awards, including a Guggenheim Fellowship, the W. Eugene Smith Award, the Legacy Award from the Smithsonian Latino Center, the Hasselblad Foundation Photography Award, and a Lucie Award for Achievement in Fine Art. In 2015 the United Nations commissioned her to photograph the plight of refugees in Mexico and Colombia.

Her photography is held in museum collections around the world. In the United States, it can be found at the J. Paul Getty Museum, Los Angeles; the San Francisco Museum of Modern Art; the California Museum of Photography, Riverside; the Museum of Fine Art, Houston; the Philadelphia Museum of Art; and the Museum of Modern Art, New York.

Iturbide resides in Mexico City, where she raised her sons, one of whom she collaborated with on *Asor*, a book loosely based on *Alice in Wonderland*. She continues to photograph as a way to understand the world in which she lives.

Further Reading

Debroise, Olivier. *Mexican Suite: A History of Photography in Mexico*. Austin: University of Texas Press, 2001.

Graciela Iturbide. www.gracielaiturbide.org.

Iturbide, Graciela. *Eyes to Fly With: Portraits, Self-Portraits, and Other Photographs*. Interview by Fabienne Bradu; foreword by Alejandro Castellanos. Austin: University of Texas Press, 2006.

Iturbide, Graciela, Elena Poniatowska, and Mario Bellatin. *Juchitán de las Mujeres, 1979–1989*. Oaxaca: Calamus Editorial, 2009.

Iturbide, Graciela, and Judith Keller. *Graciela Iturbide: Juchitán*. Los Angeles: The J. Paul Getty Museum, 2008.

Obrist, Hans Ulrich. *Conversations in Mexico*, edited by Karen Marta. Mexico City: Fundación Alumnos 47, 2016.

ISABEL QUINTERO is the daughter of Mexican immigrants. She was born and raised and currently writes and resides in the Inland Empire of Southern California. She earned her BA in English and her MA in English Composition at California State University, San Bernardino. In 2007 she visited the Getty Museum for the first time, to see the Graciela Iturbide exhibition *The Goat's Dance*. The photographs were evocative and compelling, almost like a documented mythology. And so, when in June of 2016 she received an email asking her if she'd be interested in writing a manuscript about the life of renowned photographer Graciela Iturbide, she took it as a sign and couldn't possibly say no to such an honor. Much less if she was able to work with the incredibly talented Zeke Peña, who did the cover of *Gabi, a Girl in Pieces* (Cinco Puntos Press, 2014), her first, award-winning, book. Her second book, *Ugly Cat and Pablo*, was published by Scholastic in 2017. laisabelquintero.com | @isabelinpieces

ZEKE PEÑA is a cartoonist, an illustrator, and a painter. He was born in southern New Mexico and grew up on the US–Mexico border in El Paso, Texas. He received a degree in Art History from the University of Texas at Austin and is self-taught in his studio practice. His illustrations have appeared on album and book covers, in editorials and comics, and as graphics for community organizing. His work has been exhibited at the National Museum of Mexican Art (Chicago), Albuquerque Hispanic Cultural Center, Houston Center of Photography, MACLA (San Jose), Loisaida Center (New York), El Paso Museum of Art, and Museo de Arte Ciudad Juárez, as well as galleries in the US and Mexico. In 2004, Zeke went on a backpacking trip through northern Mexico with his dad's 35-mm camera, a few rolls of black-and-white film, and a small book of Graciela Iturbide's photographs. It was a life-changing experience that Graciela's images were a part of. Twelve years later, he was excited to work with her photographs in a new way and tell her inspiring story to young people. zpvisual.com | @zpvisual

ACKNOWLEDGMENTS

We would like to thank the Getty for inviting us to be a part of such an incredible project. Thank you to Graciela Iturbide for allowing us to tell her story and to her and Oswaldo Ruiz for answering all our questions. To the Getty Museum's Department of Photographs, for opening their collection to us. To Rose Shoshana, for inviting us to her gallery at Bergamont Station and speaking to us about Graciela and her work. Thank you to Jim Drobka, Michelle Woo Deemer, Karen Levine, and everyone else at Getty Publications who worked so hard on this book.

Isabel is tremendously grateful to Mary McCoy for recommending her to this project, to Peter Steinberg for his advice, to Cinco Puntos Press for introducing her to Zeke. To Ruth Evans Lane, for her keen editing eye and for making sure that she stopped for lunch while working at the Getty Research Institute. Isabel would like to thank Zeke for his editing skills, his talent, and his saintlike patience as she learned to collaborate on a writing project and to write a graphic novel simultaneously. She'd like to thank her friends and family who all encouraged her and were excited for this project when they found out about it and listened to her talk on and on about it. To Belen Alba and Allyson Jeffredo, who sat patiently as she took phone conferences in mall parking lots or on drives or walks. Gracias a Pavel Acevedo for el apoyo. To Eric Atkinson for reading it. Lastly, gracias a sus padres Lupe y Victor, and her brother, Victor, for always loving her no matter what.

Zeke would like to thank his mom, Anna Lisa, and his late pops, Richard, for giving him life and supporting him—he still works on the drafting table they bought him when he was twelve years old. He is grateful to Isabel for thinking of him for this awesome collaboration and to Cinco Puntos Press for connecting them. He is also grateful to Ruth Evans Lane for dreaming up this project and dealing with all the frustrations that came with its insane timeline. Zeke wants to thank his partner, Rebecca Rivas, family, frontera community, and everyone who has supported him on this project and in his career. Finally, he wants to thank you and your eyeballs for reading this book.

IMAGE CAPTIONS

Many of the illustrations in this book are drawn from and inspired by the work of Graciela Iturbide—too many to list here. The Iturbide photographs reproduced in the book are listed by page number below. Those in the collection of the J. Paul Getty Museum (JPGM) are given with their accession numbers.

pp. 6–7:   *Portrait of Seri Man, Sonoran Desert*, 1979

p. 11:   *Saguaro, Sonoran Desert*, 1979
                   JPGM 2007.65.41

pp. 12–13: *Self-Portrait at My House, Mexico City*, 1974

p. 18:   *Airplane, Mexico*, about 1954

p. 22:   *Manual Álvarez Bravo, Mexico*, 1970

p. 27:   *¿Ojos para volar?, Coyoacán*, 1991

pp. 28–29: *Cemetery, Juchitán, Oaxaca*, 1988
                   JPGM 2007.65.3

p. 31:   *Rosario and Boo Boo in Their Home, East L.A.*, 1986
                   JPGM 2007.38.1

p. 33:   *Cholas, White Fence, East L.A.*, 1986

p. 35:   *Tijuana Tattoo, Tijuana*, about 1990
                   JPGM 2007.11.26

p. 39:   *Virgin Child, Ocumichu, Michoacán*, 1981
                   JPGM 2007.65.42

p. 40:   *Little Goats, La Mixteca, Oaxaca*, 1992
                   JPGM 2007.65.2

p. 43:   *The Slaughter, La Mixteca, Oaxaca*, 1992
              JPGM 2007.24.3

p. 45:   *The Sacrifice, La Mixteca, Oaxaca*, 1992
              JPGM 2007.11.27

pp. 46–47:   *Na'Lupe Pan, Juchitán, Oaxaca*, 1988
              JPGM 2007.65.34

p. 51:   *Magnolia, Juchitán, Oaxaca*, 1986
              JPGM 2007.65.26

p. 56:   *Our Lady of the Iguanas, Juchitán, Oaxaca*, 1979
              JPGM 2007.65.35

pp. 58–59:   *Highway 82: From Abbeyville to Intracoastal City, Louisiana*, 1997
              JPGM 2007.65.37.1

p. 63:   *Highway 308: From Golden Meadow to Grand Isle, Louisiana*, 1997
              JPGM 2002.70.1

p. 74:   *Untitled (Offering to Frida's Ashes), Mexico City*, 2007
              JPGM 2014.88.2

p. 78:   *Botanic Gardens, Oaxaca*, 1996–2004
              JPGM 2007.24.8

pp. 80–81:   *Tonalá, Tehuantepec, Oaxaca*, 1974
              JPGM 2007.65.32

p. 84:   *Angel Woman, Sonoran Desert*, 1979
              JPGM 2007.65.29

p. 85:   *Self-Portrait with the Seris, Sonoran Desert*, 1979

p. 88:   *Self-Portrait with Snakes, Oaxaca*, 2006

Published by the J. Paul Getty Museum, Los Angeles
Getty Publications
1200 Getty Center Drive, Suite 500
Los Angeles, CA 90049-1682
www.getty.edu/publications

Ruth Evans Lane, Editor
Jim Drobka, Designer
Michelle Woo Deemer, Production

Distributed in North America by ABRAMS, New York

Distributed outside North America by Yale University
    Press, London

Printed and bound by Great Wall Printing in Hong Kong
    (G170600032)
First printing by the J. Paul Getty Museum (15099)

Library of Congress Cataloging-in-Publication Data

Names: Quintero, Isabel, author. | Iturbide, Graciela, 1942–
    photographer. | Peña, Zeke, 1983– illustrator. | J. Paul Getty
    Museum, issuing body.
Title: Photographic : the life of Graciela Iturbide / Isabel Quintero
    and Zeke Peña.
Description: Los Angeles : J. Paul Getty Museum, [2018]
Identifiers: LCCN 2017023891 | ISBN 9781947440005
    (hardcover)
Subjects: LCSH: Iturbide, Graciela, 1942– —Juvenile
    literature. | Photography, Artistic—Juvenile literature. |
    Photographers—Mexico—Biography—Juvenile literature.
Classification: LCC TR140.I88 Q56 2017 | DDC 770.92—dc23
LC record available at https://lccn.loc.gov/2017023891

Back cover: Graciela Iturbide, *Angel Woman, Sonoran Desert*,
    1979. JPGM 2007.65.29